THE QUARTER-LIFE
BREAKTHROUGH
SMILEY POSWOLSKY

20s & 30s PRESS
SAN FRANCISCO

For anyone who ever heard, "That's not possible, you can't do that, you're not good enough, you're too young or too old, you don't have the money or the connections, it's too late," and took a deep breath, *listened to their heart, and went out and did it anyway.*

First Edition, 20s & 30s Press, April 2014

20s & 30s Press
San Francisco, California
www.thequarterlifebreakthrough.com

ISBN: 978-0-9914044-0-7
ISBN (e-book): 978-0-9914044-1-4

Edited by Caroline Kessler
Book design by Sumeet Banerji
Cover design by Bernat Fortet Unanue and Sumeet Banerji
Cover photography and headshot by Kara Brodgesell

Publisher's Cataloging-In-Publication Data

Poswolsky, Smiley.
The quarter-life breakthrough / Smiley Poswolsky. -- First edition.

pages ; cm

Issued also as an ebook.
Includes bibliographical references.
ISBN: 978-0-9914044-0-7

1. Generation Y--Employment. 2. Vocational guidance. 3. Job satisfaction. 4. Career changes. I. Title.

HF5381 .P69 2014
331.7/02/0842

Printed in the United States of America

CONTENTS

PREFACE: MY QUARTER-LIFE ~~CRISIS~~ BREAKTHROUGH · 1

INTRODUCTION · 5

PART I: ON GETTING UNSTUCK

CHAPTER 1: CHANGING YOUR CAREER MINDSET · 23

CHAPTER 2: MOVING BEYOND FOMO · 39

CHAPTER 3: EMBRACING FEAR · 51

PART II: ON FINDING MEANINGFUL WORK

CHAPTER 4: DISCOVERING MEANING · 67

CHAPTER 5: ALIGNING YOUR GIFTS WITH
YOUR IMPACT · 93

PART III: ON TAKING YOUR BREAKTHROUGH SERIOUSLY

CHAPTER 6: BREAKTHROUGH HUSTLING · 121

CHAPTER 7: GOING ALL-IN · 157

CONCLUSION: THE JOURNEY CONTINUES · 177

JOIN THE BREAKTHROUGH COMMUNITY · 181

BREAKTHROUGH HUSTLERS · 182

NOTES · 186

GRATITUDE · 191

RESOURCES · 194

PREFACE

MY QUARTER-LIFE ~~CRISIS~~ BREAKTHROUGH

Have you ever known you needed to make a change, but were completely unable to do anything about it? Have you ever felt like you were physically paralyzed by life, like you were trapped in a room and you couldn't get out?

That's exactly how I felt for almost two years at my job at the Peace Corps headquarters in Washington, D.C. On paper and to the rest of the world, the job was perfect. I worked as the special assistant to the director of global operations and later was promoted to a program specialist. I got to sit in on senior staff meetings, draft important memos, and sometimes write remarks for the director of the Peace Corps. Once, I traveled to Botswana and worked with the Secret Service to help plan Michelle Obama's visit with Peace Corps volunteers.

The job had promotion potential. I was making $70,000 a year at the age of 28. I had the best health care plan in the country, a matching 401(k) plan, and long-term job security.

My boss told me I was doing a great job, and that I was

"indispensable" to the team. My parents were proud of me. When people at happy hour asked me the D.C. requisite, "So, what do you do?" they were always impressed when I told them I worked at the Peace Corps.

Everything was perfect about my job, except for one tiny, very important thing: *I was miserable.*

Every time my alarm went off in the morning, I'd feel a shooting pain go up and down my back. I used to call this pain my "Morning Edition," because it coincided with NPR waking me up. "It's Morning Edition, for NPR News—I'm Steve Inskeep. And I'm Renée Montagne. Yesterday, the Senate blocked a measure to expand background checks for gun buyers and ban assault weapons, despite the recent tragedy at Sandy Hook Elementary School."

My Morning Edition would shoot up and down my back when I was tying my tie before leaving the house, riding the bus down 16th Street to work, and when I scanned my ID badge on the way in to the office. I'd feel it on the elevator ride upstairs, in weekly team meetings when we went over bullet-pointed to-do lists and discussed "best practices," and when I was out a bar with friends, feeling my Blackberry vibrate with an email from my boss at 10pm.

The pain, which manifested itself physically as shingles on my side (usually common among 75 year-olds, not 28 year-olds), was actually far worse emotionally. It was the pain of knowing I wasn't where I was meant to be, but having no clue where I needed to go or how to get there.

It was the pain of thinking something was wrong with me for having this great job that I wasn't energized by, a job that seemingly everyone else in my life was thrilled I had.

It was the pain of not being satisfied with working at the Peace Corps, a place that was making a positive impact in the world, whose mission was to promote world peace and friendship. I knew I wanted to help others, but if I wasn't happy at the *Peace Corps*, where the hell *would I* be satisfied working?

It was the fear that I might *never* make a change and be stuck forever in a job that wasn't right for me. It was the stress of not knowing the answers—what some people call a *quarter-life crisis*—although I certainly don't wish shingles upon the 50 million twentysomethings out there.

For over a year, I lived with my quarter-life crisis before I actually did anything about it. The experience was crippling. It was like my life was on hold. Being unhappy at work affected my ability to make simple decisions like what to eat for dinner or what to watch on Netflix. Every time I went to Target, I faced an existential crisis, because I didn't know whether I should buy a small or big bottle of shampoo, in case I decided to quit my job and move.

Receiving my monthly billing statement from Sallie Mae in my inbox made me want to throw my computer out the window. Looking at job postings on Idealist stressed me out because I had no idea what I was looking for. Seeing the cover of self-help books like *What Color is Your Parachute?, You Majored in What?,* and *Life's a Bitch and Then You Change Careers* overwhelmed me and made me nauseous.

I had a pile of career change books that I kept zipped up in a suitcase in the back of my closet because it scared me so much just to look at them. At night, I scrolled through my Facebook news feed and saw all my friends' lives unfolding and I was jealous: I wanted to be wherever they were, doing whatever they were doing.

I'd think to myself:"Maybe *I* should move to Thailand? Maybe *I* should get my MBA? Maybe *I* should start my own non-profit? Maybe *I* should work at a charter school? Maybe *I* should open my own food truck (even though I don't know how to cook). Maybe *I* should start an organic farm (even though I don't really like the smell of compost). Maybe *I* should get married and have kids (even though I don't even have a girlfriend!).

I'd lie in bed, unable to fall asleep. The choices be-sieged me. I felt helpless and alone. It was only when I met other young people going through the same thing I was going through (minus the shingles) that I realized I wasn't alone in struggling to figure out what do with my life, and felt empowered to have my breakthrough.

I wrote this book to prove it's okay to want something different than you did two years ago. It's okay to leave a job everyone else thinks is awesome, and it's okay not to know exactly what it is you want at the age of 22 (or 25 or 30 or at any point).

This is the book I wish I had during my own quarter-life crisis. This book is about how a bunch of inspiring twenty- (and thirty-) somethings changed my life, and how their stories can help change your life, too.

INTRODUCTION

When I worked at the Peace Corps, I went to a free professional development class the Office of Personnel Management was offering to employees from different government agencies. The class, called 'Establishing a Business Mindset,' was held in a fluorescent-lit basement that smelled like chlorine, in an office building somewhere on K Street in downtown Washington, D.C. The facilitator was at least 60 years old, bald and overweight, and wearing a wrinkled gray suit with dirty running shoes. He was chewing a Subway sandwich when I arrived. This immediately threw me off—who eats Subway at 9 o'clock in the morning?

At the beginning of the class, Mr. Subway asked each of us to introduce ourselves and say why we were there. There were about ten participants and I was by far the youngest in the room. One woman answered that she was interested in starting her own Internet business on the side. I went next and said, "After I leave government, I'm interested in supporting entrepreneurs who are starting ventures that are making a social impact." When I mentioned the words "leave government," I could see the eyes rolling in the room, and hear someone clear their throat.

The guy who went after me said, "Well, this is a paid staff development day, so I don't have to be in the office, which means I'm one day closer to retirement." Of the people that followed, several had the exact same answer. Another said, "I'm not at work, hallelujah."

I was surprised at how many people would attend a class about personal goal setting just to waste time, or check off another day in the long road towards their pension. But when you think about it, you can't blame them. This is how many of us are told to live our lives, either from our family or the media or even friends. This is the traditional "American Dream" retirement mindset we learn from a young age: go to college, climb the ladder, find a well-paying job that allows you to support a family, retire at 65, and you'll be fulfilled.

There's one slight problem with the retirement mindset: it doesn't actually lead to fulfillment. Gallup's 2013 State of the American Workplace report showed that as many as 70% of American workers are disengaged at their jobs. Nearly one-fifth of those people were so disengaged at the office that they were *actively undermining* their co-workers' work.[1]

I think part of this lack of fulfillment stems from our failure as a society to encourage people to ask themselves simple questions which often don't yield simple answers: *Who am I? What do I want? Why am I here? What do I want for the world? What is my purpose?* **Why?**

I've asked many of my peers *why?* over the last two years and not once has someone answered, "make lots of money so

I can buy nice stuff," "run a corporation so I can have lots of power," or "pass the time as quickly as possible, doing as little as possible, so I can retire with a pension in 40 years and go on a cruise with my partner."

Rather, they've said things like: "I want to teach urban teenagers how to avoid debt and become successful entrepreneurs," "I want to inspire young girls to think they can become engineers, and not Barbie dolls," "I want to teach kids living in a food desert how to grow their own food," and "I want to ensure large corporations reduce their carbon footprint."

Young people aren't waiting for retirement. They're asking what their purpose is *now*, and they're determined to find the opportunities, organizations, and companies that share their dreams. A recent study by Net Impact showed that the millennial generation expects to make a difference in the world through their work, and more than half of millennials would take a 15% pay cut to do work for an organization that matches their values.[2]

Millennials (in this book, used to describe those born in the 1980s and 1990s) are not alone in choosing meaning as more important than money in their lives. Studies have shown that increased salary, after more than $75,000 annually, doesn't correlate to happiness or emotional well-being.[3]

Regardless of where you're coming from, there are several assumptions I'm making about where you're going. If *any* of these assumptions apply to you, this book is for you. First, **you refuse to settle for mediocrity.** You want to spend your days doing something that inspires you. Second, **you want to make a positive difference in the lives of others.** Whether you want to solve a pressing social problem or make someone feel better about her day, you want to make an impact. And finally, **you're prepared to take action.** You know that the hardest part is starting the journey, but you're ready to begin making changes now.

My friend Nate recently left his job to pursue his venture, The Loveumentary, a podcast, blog, and book that shares stories about true love and healthy relationships. He explains his transition by saying, "I'd rather spend my days working on something I feel incredibly inspired by and proud of, than to waste it in a job counting down the minutes till I can go home. I decided that if I didn't like my life how it was, it was my job to change it, and so I did."

We spend nearly half our waking lives working.[4] This book is for everyone who feels like Nate, who wants to reach their potential, spend their days working with purpose, and find meaningful work (as opposed to mediocre work).

Mediocre work is a job that pays the bills. It's something that passes the time, work you're not fully engaged with or interested in, for a cause or company that doesn't align with what you care about. Mediocre work may add to your financial well-being, but doesn't allow you to make your unique contribution to the world.

In contrast, this book contends that **meaningful work**

provides personal meaning, reflecting who you are and what your interests are, allows you to share your gifts to help others, and is financially viable given your desired lifestyle. I'll spend time later on in the book dissecting this definition, and having you create a specific definition of what meaningful work is for you.

Viktor Frankl's bestselling and still-relevant book, *Man's Search for Meaning* is about his experience in a Nazi concentration camp, during which he lost his pregnant wife and most of his family. Frankl wrote: "Being human always points, and is directed, to something or someone, other than oneself—be it a meaning to fulfill or another human being to encounter. The more one forgets himself— by giving himself to a cause to serve or another person to love—the more human he is."[5]

Although there are multiple ways to define 'meaning,' I interpret Frankl's words to define meaning as something that comes not from personal gain, but from service or companionship, from positively impacting the lives of others.

Let's be real: it's hard enough for young people to find *any job* in today's job market. Finding meaningful work is even more challenging. According to the Pew Research Center, only 54% of American adults ages 18 to 25 are currently employed, the lowest percentage since the government began collecting data sixty years ago.[6] The U.S. nonemployment rate (which includes the unemployed and those who have dropped out of the labor force) among 25-34 year-olds is over 25%.[7]

Since 1983 (the year I was born), the average net worth of someone between the ages of 29 and 37 has fallen over 20%.[8] One in four adults between 18 and 34 years old say they have moved back in with their parents after living on their own.[9] Breaking from tradition, our generation may grow up to be *less* wealthy than our parents' generation.[10]

Every generation probably feels like it has gotten the short end of the stick, but critics really love to hate on millennials. They call us the lazy generation, the entitled generation, and the "me me me generation."[11] Based on the young people I know and the ones you'll read about in this book, these stereotypes couldn't be farther from the truth. Millennials want to work—and despite being shackled by debt, recession, and the jobs crisis—they aren't motivated by money. Rather, they're driven to make the world more compassionate, innovative, and sustainable.

We aren't the "me me me generation." We're a group of determined individuals who refuse to settle because we know how great our impact can be when we find work we truly care about. Most books and articles about twentysomethings focus on the *problem*: why we are doomed, in debt, depressed, lazy, unlucky, entitled, or addicted to Facebook. Instead, I wrote about the *solution*, so that anyone going through a quarter-life crisis can turn a moment of being stuck into a **breakthrough**, *a moment of opportunity and possibility when you discover why you're doing what you're doing and what you want to give to the world.*

As part of my journey over the last eighteen months, I became a StartingBloc Fellow, completing a program that trains emerging leaders to drive social innovation across sectors and fosters a tight-knit community of changemakers in 55 countries. I mentored at Dell's Summer Social Innovation Lab, an institute for talented social entrepreneurs that teaches proven strategies in transformative action, design, and business. I also directed The Bold Academy, an intensive, residential leadership development program for young professionals interested in finding clarity, building confidence, and working with purpose.

During this time, I interviewed and met with more than 100 highly-motivated millennials. Some of them quit their jobs to start their own ventures, some now work for the world's most innovative companies, and some are still figuring out the next step in their breakthroughs. My goal in capturing these stories was to discover *how we can each get a little bit closer to knowing why we're doing what we're doing and take action towards reaching our potential.*

This book shares the stories of many twenty- (and thirty-) somethings who are figuring out how to work with purpose (and still pay their rent). The goal of this book is to help you find purposeful work, work that makes you come alive and feel excited to start your day, even on a Monday morning (or at least most Monday mornings). Reading this book will help you get a little closer to who you are and discovering what your next step might be in the context of building a purposeful career.

That next step might be quitting your current job, finding a new job, or embarking on an entirely new career path. It might be deciding whether to go to graduate school, pursue a project you've been dreaming about, or start your own business. The next step may seem small at first: experimenting with things that interest you, learning a new skill, and finding communities who will hold you accountable to your dreams. Or it might mean accepting that you don't know what the next step will be.

This book won't tell you what you should do with your life (how would I know? I've never even met you!). It won't tell you to find "the perfect job" (how it is possible to know what your "perfect job" is before you've lived your life?). And it won't tell you to work only four hours a week (why would you want to avoid something that might fulfill you?). **It will simply empower you to get closer to finding a job or opportunity that allows you to share your gifts and make a positive impact in the lives of others**.

Finding meaningful work is by no means easy, but it's not impossible either. Unlike 70% of Americans, the millennials profiled in this book are excited about how they spend their days. They've done everything from register thousands of first-time voters to start an urban farm, leave a non-profit for a tech company, and leave a tech company for a non-profit (and tons more in between). Any kind of work can be meaningful: the challenge is discovering *what in particular makes you come alive*.

Finding meaningful work requires asking many

personal questions before it rewards any answers. Finding the work that makes you come alive is all about alignment and fit. What works for your friend may not work for you. You can have the wrong job at the right organization, or the right job at the wrong organization, or even the wrong job at the wrong organization.

Additionally, your purpose is constantly evolving as you learn new things, travel to new places, make new friends, start families, raise children, build communities, and grow older. What was purposeful for you one year may no longer be purposeful for you a few years later.

This book is divided into three parts, reflecting three stages in any quarter-life breakthrough.

In **Part I**, you'll start by taking small steps. I'll share the story of how I've had eight jobs since college, and argue that climbing a career ladder limits the potential for risk-taking and experimentation, and is impractical in today's rapidly evolving and unstable job market. Instead of moving up and down on a ladder, we'll think of careers as a series of lily pads, extending in all directions, which allow you to jump to any new project or opportunity based on your purpose. You'll embrace the journey by moving beyond FOMO (Fear of Missing Out), listening when a light goes off telling you something isn't right, and using fear to guide you in the right direction.

In **Part II**, you'll create your own definition of meaningful work. You'll discover how to align your work with your purpose and how to kick-start your job search by trying on jobs to see if they fit through short-term experiences and apprenticeships. We'll talk about balancing money and meaning, and how to determine your priorities. If graduate school is on your radar, we'll find out from several recent law school and business school graduates how to figure out whether grad school is "worth it" for you, and whether now is the right time for you to go back to school.

And finally, in **Part III**, you'll get your breakthrough hustle on and take action towards getting what you want. You'll start by practicing self-love and prioritizing the things that make you happy. You'll do short exercises, which will help you go outside your comfort zone and accomplish your six-month goals. You'll brainstorm ways to invest in your breakthrough and build a supportive community of people who share your values. Based on the stories of people like you who have recently had breakthroughs, you'll learn useful lessons in breakthrough hustling that will help you make an impact today and going forward.

An introduction wouldn't be complete without a few important caveats.

Life is more than "what you do"

We live in a society that likes to define us by our job titles, how much money we make, who we know, and how cool our business card looks. While I lived in Washington, D.C., I grew accustomed to answering the requisite "So, what do you do?" wherever I went. In fact, I once met a woman at happy hour who asked me for my business card before she even shook my hand or got my name—as if our interaction hinged on my job title.

I hated answering this question for a couple reasons. First, because telling someone my position, "I'm the special assistant **to the** director of global operations at the U.S. Peace Corps," kind of made me feel like Dwight Schrute talking to Michael Scott in *The Office.*

Second, because it didn't really describe who I was. It left out all the fun stuff—like the fact that my favorite thing to do in the world is sip coffee and write in my Moleskine, or that if it was up to me, I'd eat a bagel with lox and cream cheese every meal for the rest of my life, or that I have seen every single episode of *Seinfeld* fourteen times, and cannot have a conversation—even on a date—without busting into my Kramer voice (*"Oh, I'm stressed…"*).

Telling someone what I did for a living also didn't describe the people in my life who I love most. It left out my role model, my younger sister, who I talk to every day about life decisions as serious as whether she should go to law school and as trivial as whether it's appropriate for me to wear running shoes on an OkCupid date. My job title doesn't include how grateful I am for my loving parents and my friends, who make me laugh so hard I usually end up on the floor whenever I'm with them.

"What you do" matters—that's why you're reading this book—but life is more than a job. The time we spend outside the office, doing things we love with people we care about is where many find fulfillment. However, since I'm 30 years old, live with five roommates in an apartment with a mouse problem, recently attended a singles yoga class, and am still wearing running shoes and talking like Kramer on dates, I decided to write this book about something I can actually speak to: my journey over the last ten years to find meaningful work.

Having said that, I hope that some of the strategies to plan your breakthrough and become mindful about how you spend your days will bring you closer to the types of people and experiences that provide true joy and fulfillment, inside and outside of the workplace.

Being able to choose "what you do" is a rare gift

On Tuesday evenings, I volunteer at the juvenile hall in San Francisco with a non-profit called The Beat Within. I facilitate writing workshops and help provide a safe space for self-expression for teenage kids who are incarcerated. There are some 70,000 young people in juvenile detention or correctional facilities every day in the United States. Nearly 3 out of 4 youth confined for delinquency are not in for a serious violent felony crime.[12]

Some of the kids we work with will go on to complete high school and attend college, get jobs, and raise families. But despite being talented poets, writers, and artists, many of them will spend the majority of their lives in and out of the criminal justice system. It's a vicious cycle, but not uncommon for people, especially black men growing up in low-income communities.

Listening to their stories, and what many have been through at a young age—including loss of family and exposure to traumatic violence—makes it easy to recognize the freedom and privilege I take for granted in my everyday life in San Francisco.

Everyone deserves the chance to find meaningful work—*everyone*. However, the harsh reality is that most people wake up every day without the ability to decide what they do for a living. Nearly half the world's population—more than 3 billion people—live on less than $2.50 a day.[13] At least 1.2 billion people live in extreme poverty, lacking access to basic needs like clean drinking water, food, and sanitation services.[14] Millions more, including in the United States, lack the financial ability, the access to education and health care, civil and human rights, or the physical freedom to make these choices.

Being able to choose what you do with your life is an enormous privilege, and it shouldn't be wasted. This doesn't mean everyone who went to college and owns a MacBook should rush off to work in an impoverished African village, or that people with relative means are necessarily happier than people without (some research suggests otherwise). But it does mean those of us fortunate enough to decide what we do should think deeply about we care about, how we want to use the time we have, and how we can each leave this world a little better than we found it.

Reading this book is just the beginning

The last time I picked up a career change book, I put it down after two minutes and hid it in my closet. That terrifying book was 373 pages, full of intimidating goal charts and worksheets that looked like something from the SAT, and full of statistics and case studies of how famous, rich people like Bill Gates and Mark Zuckerberg started their careers.

Instead of writing a book like the ones I hid in my closet, I decided to write a short book without too many statistics, but with a lot of fun exercises, helpful resources, and engaging stories of young people figuring out what to do with their lives. Here's how to get the most out of this book:

- **Do the exercises.** Throughout the book you'll find practical exercises and reflections intended to help you at each stage of your breakthrough. These are meant to be fun, useful, and as un–SAT as possible. You may find it helpful to have a journal or sketchbook close by, in case you want to jot down any ideas. If some of the exercises don't work for you, skip them. Come back to them later (just don't hide this book in your closet!).

- **Use the resources section.** This book is a quick read for a reason, but reading it won't answer all your questions. It's only the beginning. The Resources section has everything from job boards to self-discovery books that will help you on your path.

- **Share your story.** The gifted twenty- and thirty-somethings whose stories I tell didn't start companies like Microsoft and Facebook. They're not famous, and they're definitely not rich. They're my friends who I love, who have inspired me to dream bigger. All of them are still figuring it out, like you and me. Each has failed and succeeded in some way or another. By the end of this book, I hope you'll share your own narrative of what you want for the world, just like my friends did.

Everyone is different. There is no right answer or cure-all when it comes to finding meaningful work. The people who find it are the ones who spend time looking for it. *The only person who knows what is right for you is you.* No self-help author (especially one nicknamed Smiley), career counselor, life coach, parent, boss, acronym-prone personality test, GRE, LSAT, or GMAT score, or friend's Facebook post can start making these decisions for you.

You have to start sometime, so how about right now?!

PART I
ON GETTING UNSTUCK

"Not all those who wander are lost."
–J. R. R. Tolkien

CHANGING YOUR CAREER MINDSET

One of the things taped above my desk is an article from *The Onion* with the headline, "24-Year-Old Receives Sage Counsel From Venerable 27-Year-Old," and a picture of two twentysomethings in plaid shirts in deep existential conversation over pints of beer at a bar.[15]

When I told my dad I was writing a career advice book, he looked at me like I was crazy, and asked, "What qualifies *you* to be writing a book about careers? You've changed what you wanted to do with your life every other year since you were a kid."

My dad is absolutely right. I've never been able to focus on any one thing for very long, and I still have trouble answering the question, "What do you want to be when you grow up?" At first, I wanted to be Big Bird, road-tripping around the country in *Follow That Bird*. Then I wanted to be Mister Rogers. Once, my family was staying at a hotel, and Fred Rogers was there having breakfast. I ran right up to him and exclaimed, "Excuse me, Mister Rogers, Mister Rogers! How did you get out of the TV?!"

When I was in 4th grade, I wanted to be a play-by-play announcer for the Olympics. In 8th grade, I wanted to be Adam Sandler. In high school, I wanted to be a sports writer. Then I went to a liberal arts college, which is to say I majored in film studies, studied abroad in Cuba, and took intro to dance senior year. Making career choices has proved difficult ever since.

After graduation, I could write a 15-page shot-by-shot analysis of David Lynch's *Mulholland Drive* and tell you the difference between cage-free, free-range, and pasture-raised eggs. But I realized college had not prepared me for the job-finding process in the slightest. Since I had no idea which "career ladder" to climb, I moved to the city where all my friends were moving (Brooklyn), and got a job that matched my college major (film), which is what I thought I was supposed to do at the time.

In the eight years since graduation, I've had eight drastically different jobs, lived in six cities, and gone down four career paths. I've never once seen this elusive "career ladder" everyone talks about. But I do know that whoever invented the ladder has been freaking twentysomethings out for a long time.

Where do you get on the ladder? Is there one in each city in the world? If you hop off for a detour, do you have to start back from the bottom, or do you get to keep your place in line? Is there music along the way, is it like Pandora, can I choose my station?

As insufferable as this ladder mindset can be, twentysomethings are still erringly being told to maintain a linear career trajectory. Even my father, who was born in the 1950s, hasn't followed any sort of career path. He has worked in stage management and lighting design for off-off-Broadway shows, then for a rock 'n' roll theater start-up in London, dropped out of NYU's theater school, sailed across the Atlantic, joined Pink Floyd as a roadie doing lighting on their international tours, became disenchanted with life on the road and enrolled in architecture school, worked as an architect, raised kids, spent time in corporate real estate, got his MBA at the age of 53, built dialysis clinics, and managed projects and workplace innovation for a large electronics company. Yet even he was skeptical when I told him I wasn't pursuing a "traditional" career path after college, and instead was headed to New York to freelance on film sets.

If you've struggled with picking a career path, or focusing on one interest or calling, then you're not alone. Only 27% of college graduates have a job related to their college major.[16]

In high school and during college, I scooped ice cream at Ben & Jerry's, had a few stints as a barista, and among other things, worked at a garden shop, helping customers pick out shade perennials (pretending that I actually knew what a shade perennial was). To list all of my high school and college jobs would be overwhelming. Here's the eclectic array of jobs I've held since graduating from college.

My Wandering Journey

Age   *Job + Motivation*

18   **Student at Wesleyan University** (Middletown, CT)
Make friends, protest George W. Bush, gain liberal
arts education

22   **Move back home with parents** (Cambridge, MA)
Unemployed and broke

22   **Freelance film location scout** (Brooklyn, NY)
Live with best friends in Brooklyn, I majored in film,
I love movies

25   **Film Festival assistant** (Buenos Aires, Argentina)
Live in Argentina, learn Spanish, travel

26   **Obama '08 campaign organizer** (Anderson, IN)
Join change movement, support gay marriage, keep
John McCain from destroying the world

26   **Waiter at Eatonville restaurant** (Washington, D.C.)
Make money to pay rent, I love food and people

27   **Move back home with parents** (Cambridge, MA)
Unemployed and broke

27   **Special Assistant at Peace Corps** (Washington, D.C.)
Believe in Peace Corps' mission to promote world
peace and friendship

30   **Freelance writer & Bold Academy director** (SF, CA)
Live in San Francisco, I love to write, support
social entrepreneurs, help young people
have breakthroughs

There are two mindsets through which one could analyze my "career" up to this point. The first is what I'll call the **career ladder mindset**, the one we've been taught to follow most of our lives. This mindset tells us that the more AP classes we take, the better we do on our SATs, the better college we go to, the more money we make, the higher on the ladder we rise, the more successful we are.

Someone with this mindset would look at my career and say, "This kid Smiley is a hot mess, he lived at his parents' house at the age of 27! He can't make up his mind. He won't stay in a job for more than two years. He'll never be successful because he's not on a specific career ladder. Think of where he could have been if he had spent the last eight years in film."

Although recent college graduates are often encouraged to adopt a career ladder mindset, these career ladders have several essential flaws:

- **Career ladders limit new opportunities, experimentation, and risk-taking**. What happens if an amazing opportunity presents itself—say, to join the 2008 Obama campaign—and I want to get off the ladder, but I've already spent two years on a different career? Ladders encourage people to avoid new challenges in exchange for safety and "moving up." Avoiding these risks may mean avoiding the very opportunities that provide us the greatest satisfaction in life. If there isn't only one answer, there probably isn't one "top of the ladder," either.

- **Career ladders define success on someone else's terms, not my own.** Career ladders lead to promotion potential and higher salary. The theory is, "Pay your dues early, and you'll reap the benefits later." I'm not a huge fan of delayed gratification in general—not many millennials are—but it's especially annoying when I don't even get to define what my gratification is or what success means to me. What happens if I'm not in it for a fancy job title or a big salary? What happens if success for me is not my retirement package at 65, but one person realizing their life potential from a blog post I write?

- **Career ladders make me stress about the future, which inhibits me from taking action now.** When I was thinking about leaving my job at the Peace Corps, one of the things I was interested in pursuing next was writing. Whenever I brought up the possibility of becoming a freelance writer, all I heard from people was, "Well, it's a hard career ladder to climb. You can't get a staff writing position at a major newspaper anymore. Newspapers don't even exist. *The New Yorker* receives 100,000 submissions an hour."

To some degree, the people warning me not to go into freelance writing at the age of 28 were right: writing is extremely competitive, and it's the opposite of financially lucrative. But stressing about my future career as a writer and about where I'd end up ten or twenty years down the road *nearly stopped me from even trying.* I hadn't even written a blog post yet, and I was thinking about writing for *The New Yorker.* I was stressing about the future, instead of taking action now.

The best advice I got about starting a writing career was from my friend Ryan Goldberg, a freelance journalist who lives in Brooklyn and has numerous bylines in *The New York Times.* At the time we talked, Ryan was also refereeing dodgeball to supplement his income. He told me, "Smiley, if you want to be a writer, write. Start writing, today."

The other of way of looking at my career is through what I'll call the **breakthrough career mindset**, which my friend and career strategist Nathaniel Koloc compares to lily pads. Nathaniel founded ReWork, a talent firm that places purpose-seeking professionals in social impact jobs. He has made it his job to study how people build careers worth having. He sometimes describes careers as *a series of lily pads*, extending in all directions. Each lily pad is a job or opportunity that's available, and *you can jump in any direction that makes sense for you, given your purpose* (how you want to help the world).

Nathaniel says, "There is no clear way 'up' anymore, it's just a series of projects or jobs, one after another. You can move in any direction, the only question is how you're devising your strategy of where to move and where you can 'land,' i.e., what you're competitive for." [17]

Leaping to another lily pad for a new job or opportunity doesn't mean you're going backwards. There is no backwards. It means you're getting closer to wherever your roots, your purpose, and your interests are pulling you. The breakthrough career mindset argues that motivated people who want to align their work with their purpose *should consider frequent small career jumps based on their changing purpose and interests.* This is especially important in a difficult job market that requires job seekers to constantly evolve and develop new skills to remain competitive.

Someone with the breakthrough career mindset would look at my career thus far and say, "Smiley is a curious guy who has a number of different interests: film, political organizing, public service, and writing. These interests have allowed him to leap to several different lily pads. He's worked on a Hollywood movie, been the only American working for a film festival in Argentina, helped Barack Obama become the first Democratic presidential candidate to win Indiana since 1964, represented the Peace Corps in high-level meetings at the White House, and started a blog that over 30,000 people have read. Rather than spending his twenties pursuing one interest or one purpose, this decade has given him a range of work experiences in different settings. This reflects a desire to help others through writing, storytelling, and creating transformative experiences for others."

Instead of one ladder leading straight up, the **breakthrough career mindset** visualizes your career as a *pond of lily pads, a series of interconnecting leaps you've made between different opportunities.* What's holding everything together is the *roots, what you care about and how you want to help the world.* In my case, today my roots are driving me to inspire others through storytelling and creating experiences to help others realize their full potential. Your roots may be driving you to do one thing now, but that thing may change in five years.

Our new economy is characterized by rapid technological innovation. How we communicate and how we work are constantly changing in an increasingly global job market. Whether they want to or not, fewer and fewer people are staying in one job for a long period of time. The average American stays at her job for about four years, and over 90% of millennials expect to stay in a job for less than three years.[18]

In an article about "Generation Flux," and how to succeed in this new business climate, Robert Safian, editor of *Fast Company*, argues that we need a mindset that embraces instability and recalibrating careers. "Our institutions are out of date," he writes. "The long career is dead; any quest for solid rules is pointless, since we will be constantly rethinking them; you can't rely on an established business model or a corporate ladder to point your way; silos between industries are breaking down; anything settled is vulnerable."[19]

Embrace The Journey

Many career paths that provided long-term job security for our parents no longer exist. But a breakthrough career mindset allows us to get closer to finding meaningful work because we can experiment with a variety of opportunities to find the right fit.

The story of my friend Alex is a brilliant illustration of the breakthrough career mindset. He's a gifted writer who used to work as a journalist for Major League Baseball. His beat was the Boston Red Sox, and he covered their exciting

World Series victory in 2007.

Like every other young kid growing up in Boston, Massachusetts, I dreamed of playing for the Red Sox. I acted out every single position at Fenway: pitcher, batter, the play-by-play announcer, the third base coach spitting tobacco, the guy in the stands selling Cracker Jacks. My mom even made me a catcher's mask out of my sister's Barbie lawn chair.

I used to run around the backyard over and over again; *Red Sox down by 3, bases loaded, bottom of the ninth, three balls and two strikes, Poswolsky's up to bat. And there's a drive deep to left…way back, way back…and it's…it's…it's….over the Green Monster!*

Alex, too, was a baseball fan. "I didn't just grow up playing and watching baseball—I was a die-hard baseball *nerd*," he remembers. "My idea of a perfect summer afternoon was to memorize the midseason MLB stats and predict the All-Star teams before they were even picked. And I loved sports writing—I was reading *Sports Illustrated* cover-to-cover by the time I was out of elementary school."

So when he told me he left quite possibly the coolest sports writing job *ever*, I thought he was nuts. I was actually personally *offended*. My childhood self would have thrown my Barbie lawn chair catcher's mask down in disgust.

But then Alex explained to me that he was tired of spending an hour after every game in a locker room full of jocks taking painkillers and icing themselves. Moreover, he wanted to contribute to something greater than himself. He left his job at MLB.com to volunteer on the 2008 Obama campaign.

Alex quit his job because something in his heart was telling him to make a change. Something about the way he was spending his days wasn't working. He made a decision based on his own priorities (not what another baseball fan would say) and ignored the misconception that career choices have to be linear (he went from sports writing to political organizing).

People change. So should what they do for a living. "I came of age during the Bush presidency and the Iraq War," Alex recalls. "Obama was clearly a page-turn. I read his memoir, which got me thinking about how much his values seemed to square with mine. So I thought, what the hell. I started volunteering. Eventually, I was hired as a field organizer. The campaign put me in touch with a side of my home city (Birmingham, Alabama) and the South, that I probably never would have had a chance to see otherwise. By working in areas of the South where voters and volunteers didn't have health insurance or a living wage and lived without electricity; that experience really stuck with me."

Alex worked in seven states, slept in the homes of countless volunteers, and was responsible for registering some 25,000 first-time voters in the Southeast, helping Obama defeat McCain by a landslide.

When we stop thinking about career choices as a race to the top or to some "perfect job" and instead as pond of lily pads to leap between, our chances for ongoing fulfillment drastically improve.

After working on the Obama campaign, Alex moved

to Washington, D.C. to work for a senior official in the Office of Management and Budget. After two years, he was eager to get back into writing, so he moved to New York and managed social media for the U.S. Ambassador to the United Nations. During the spring of 2013, after two years at the UN, he was ready for another change. He decided to move out west to San Francisco to work on executive communications at Google.

Someone with the career ladder mindset might criticize a person for having five different jobs in four cities in six years. Someone with the breakthrough career mindset commends Alex for his *flexibility* and *experimentation*. Alex gained communications experience in sports, government, foreign policy, and the technology sector, trying to find the right fit while working on issues he cared about. In the meantime, he's built a pretty impressive resume.

Alex is enjoying working at Google. But knowing him, I imagine he might tire of the free coconut water after a couple of years, and move on to another exciting opportunity that aligns with how he wants to spend his days. Shit, maybe he'll even go back to writing about baseball. And that is perfectly okay.

"Smiley, wait—I haven't even had my first quarter-life breakthrough yet, and you're already telling me I should expect more than one?" Yes. *Accept that there probably isn't only one answer, and explore multiple answers.*

This doesn't mean you have to change jobs or move

cities every other year (you may find that your next transition brings you somewhere you stay for many years, or even your entire career), but it does mean you'll have to frequently *consider* your changing purpose and interests, to get closer to what you want for yourself and the world.

The journey is the journey—there is no finish line, no top of the ladder. Your career is simply a series of journeys. Some may be tiny pivots. Others may be huge leaps. Embrace this journey that you're on today. As my friend and yoga teacher Julia Winston, reminds me, "We run forward, we push, we have goals, we dream, to get to the present." (No, Julia is not my singles yoga teacher. That guy doesn't talk about the journey, he plays Marvin Gaye's "Let's Get It On" during savasana.)

Career Experimentation vs. Wasting Time

What's the difference between career experimentation and wasting time? I know they can look eerily similar sometimes. I didn't write this book so young people could avoid worrying about the future. I wrote it so they could feel empowered to *take tangible steps right now toward working with purpose.*

There's an excellent TED talk called "Why 30 is not the new 20," by clinical psychologist Meg Jay, author of *The Defining Decade: Why Your Twenties Matter--And How to Make the Most of Them Now.* The book is based on her work with numerous young people experiencing quarter-life crises. In her book and TED talk, she argues that one of the reasons that half of all twentysomethings are un-employed or underemployed is that many avoid taking their twenties seriously. Because they put off important decisions about personal identity, career, and family, they end up facing more serious life crises when they're older.[20]

I agree—at least about the personal identity and career part. I can't really speak about settling down and raising a family yet, since I'm still going to singles yoga. *The time for intentional learning, experimentation, and action is now.*

The breakthrough career mindset doesn't say "your twenties don't matter," or "don't worry about your career until you're older." On the contrary, I'm advocating that you should take advantage of opportunities when they present themselves, and thoroughly explore different career options to get closer to who you are, what you value, and how you want to help others.

What sense would it have made for me to stay in government if I was tired of working in government, just to wait for retirement in 35 years? None. Just like it would have made no sense for Alex to keep writing about baseball when he was ready to jump onto a political campaign he believed in.

Build a purposeful career by experimenting with opportunities you actually care about. This isn't wasting your twenties or thirties—it's making them count.

REMEMBER

If you want to change jobs or start down a new career path, the time to begin is now. The career ladder is an outdated metaphor that may have been practical in a job market of our parents' generation, where there were more jobs you could stay in for longer periods of time. But today's evolving job market rewards those with a wide range of skills and experiences, who are curious, resourceful, and inventive. Motivated and purpose-driven people make frequent career jumps based on their changing interests and desires in order maximize their impact.

If the majority of millennials expect to stay in a job for less than three years, then that means some of us will have as many as 15 or even 20 jobs in our lifetime. That's a lot of time spent job hunting and freaking out. Where do you even start? By taking a deep breath and pressing onwards. In Chapter 2, you'll learn how to stop comparing yourself to others, and start listening to your true self, which will help you explore what makes you come alive, and discover the right lily pad to jump to next.

MOVING BEYOND FOMO

During my quarter-life crisis (shingles and all), I felt paralyzed to make a change. I felt like I was at the intersection of hopeless, stuck, and FOMO-dosed (Fear of Missing Out-overdosed).

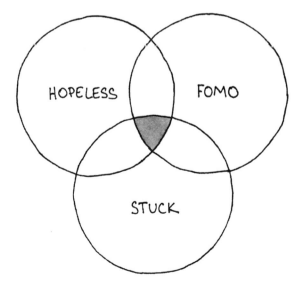

I told myself the following:

Hopeless: "I wish I could do _____. But that's impossible, I'd never be able to do that. They're no jobs available in that field. It would take years to do that. It's too late to do that, I'm already 28."

FOMO-dosed: "All my friends on Facebook are so happy and successful. I'm so jealous. I want to do what they're doing. Some of my friends are lawyers now—that's nuts! A kid I went to college with was nominated for an Oscar! My friend started a company, and he's a *Forbes* 30 Under 30. Wow, my buddy is traveling around Southeast Asia. I feel so boring. Everyone is getting engaged—I'm tired of being single."

Stuck: "I hate my job. I want to do something else, but I don't know where to start. I'm interested in so many things, but none of them seem perfect. There are too many choices of what I could do next. I'm overwhelmed, stressed, and all I want to do is watch *Arrested Development* on Netflix. Or maybe *Mad Men*. I can't even decide which *TV show* to watch."

Everything feels impossible during a quarter-life crisis, even small decisions like which size shampoo to buy or which TV show to watch. But to truly embrace the journey means you need to truly change your perspective, from helplessness to possibility.

In this chapter, you'll learn three easy steps to adopt a **breakthrough perspective**, a perspective that says: *Rather than feel like everything is impossible, I'm going to* *take tangible steps and start exploring what I'm interested in.*

If you're feeling hopeless, FOMO'dosed, stuck, or any combination of those three, there are some clear ways to begin changing your perspective: express gratitude, stop comparing yourself to others, and listen to your true self. Having a breakthrough perspective will help you start exploring your interests so you can jump to the next lily pad in your journey towards meaningful work.

Hopeless ➔ EXPRESS GRATITUDE

I learned about what really matters in life from my grandmother. Gran grew up during the Depression, when her family lost everything they had. She learned to take pleasure from the smallest things in life, like drinking coffee, reading *The New York Times*, and eating bacon cheeseburgers. After her husband died when my father was young, she decided not to remarry, and lived by herself in the same one-bedroom apartment in Greenwich Village for over fifty years.

When she was in her 80s, Gran was hit by a taxicab while crossing the street in a crosswalk near Union Square. But the accident didn't stop her—she worked full-time until the age of 84, as a bookkeeper for an advertising firm in Manhattan. She enjoyed walking to work in the morning, and took pride in managing the firm's money, learning how to use a computer and QuickBooks, and being the oldest woman in the office.

When I lived in New York after college, I used to go to her apartment every Friday. She would sit on her red reading chair with white polka dots, and tell me that the most meaningful moments in her life were spending time with my sister and I when we were kids. We played a game called "Restaurant," where Gran would lie in bed and read the paper, while my sister and I would take her order and then pretend to cook the food in the kitchen.

"You have no idea how much joy you kids brought me," Gran told me one Friday. "And to think, I didn't even have to stand up." Toward the end of her life, when Gran got really sick, the pain became too much and she said it was no longer pleasant for her to be alive. She called herself a "hospice reject" because she couldn't die, and when I'd ask her if I could get her anything, she'd joke, "a knife."

I often imagine Gran sitting in her apartment on her red reading chair, one of the last times we were together, saying, "I'm very happy just sitting here with you, Adam. That's all I ever needed." She made me feel like no matter what shit the world throws at you (even old age and death), I still have something to smile about. Whenever I stress about the future (which is to say, pretty much every day), I remember Gran and the other people I'm grateful for in my life.

BREAKTHROUGH EXERCISE

Express Gratitude

Make a list of five people you're grateful for—they could be family, friends, partners, children, or colleagues. Write a few sentences about why you're grateful for each person. Next time you see them, let them know how much they mean to you. If they live far away, send them a postcard or letter expressing your gratitude.

FOMO'dosed ➜ STOP COMPARING YOURSELF WITH OTHERS

Social media has made it all but impossible to avoid comparing yourself to others. We only see the coolest parts of our friends' lives, like when they get a new job, fall in love, or travel somewhere beautiful. We think, "Wow, I really need to get my shit together."

All of us are figuring it out, even our friends whose Facebook grass looks *really* green. All of us are on different paths, with no right or wrong answer. Comparing yourself to others is a waste of time.

My friend Kristen McKee recently left her sales job at Google, where she worked for over five years. She held off quitting for an entire year after deciding she wanted to leave, due to a mix of guilt and uncertainty. Several of her friends and family desperately wanted to work at Google, and she knew she was lucky to have landed her dream job right after college. She told me, "Something inside me knew I could make a more meaningful impact elsewhere, doing things that energized me instead of drained me, and I finally realized that feeling guilty was not a good reason to stay at my job."

By moving beyond worrying about what *other* people thought of her job, Kristen was able to do what many people never do: start figuring out what *she* wanted. Since leaving Google, she's invested in her personal development at The Bold Academy and The Landmark Forum, a program that helps people transform their relationships, communication, productivity, and leadership potential. She strengthened her professional network at the World Domination Summit, an annual gathering of over 3,000 entrepreneurs and artists interested in changing the world. She also pursued her love for writing, art, and personal health. She launched a blog, contributed content to numerous websites, showed her paintings in two art shows in Portland, and is now training to become an Intensati exercise instructor, as well as pursuing her esthetician certification with the plan to open her own spa one day.

Needless to say, Kristen isn't sure exactly which lily pad she'll be on in two years, but she has embraced the journey to explore herself and what energizes her. She has adopted a **breakthrough perspective**: rather than tell herself everything she's interested in doing is impossible, she's taking small steps to explore her many interests.

It's important to realize that having a breakthrough perspective means *exploring* what you're interested in. But exploring and experimenting with your interests doesn't necessarily mean starting your own business or quitting your job tomorrow. By taking *tangible steps* towards things you're interested in, you can get closer to discovering how you want to share your gifts with the world. By launching a blog, contributing content to a few websites, and signing up for an esthetician certification class, Kristen has begun to figure out what lily pad she should jump to next. We'll talk more in later chapters about what tangible steps you can take to explore your own interests.

Kristen is now a third of the way through her esthetician certification at Aveda Institute. She has already taken on several clients for various services, and has done makeup at a black tie runway show and an advertising firm's Halloween party. "It turns out I *love* working with clients in such a hands-on, nurturing industry," Kristen explains. "I never knew how much I love doing makeup until now, and it's all because I took the step to get this certification. Making people feel beautiful and comfortable in their own skin is a gift of mine; I think it really combines the artist and caretaker in me."

The journey is personal. Finding meaning is about looking within and listening to the voice inside.

> ## BREAKTHROUGH EXERCISE
>
> ### Social Media Sabbatical
>
> In order to stop worrying about what *other* people think and start figuring out what *you* want, take a one-week social media sabbatical, beginning next Monday. Don't check your Facebook, Twitter, or Instagram until the following Monday. Trust me: you can do it and it's not impossible. I've done it for a month and survived. If you have to use social media for work, avoid your personal accounts. During your sabbatical, try experimenting daily with a creative activity that you love to do, like writing in your journal, painting, or drawing.

Stuck → LISTEN TO YOUR TRUE SELF

The first part of any quarter-life breakthrough is when a light goes off, alerting you that something in your life isn't working. I'll never forget the moment when my light went off.

In February 2012, I went to a five-day leadership training program called StartingBloc that focuses on social innovation for purpose-driven professionals. At the program in southern California, I met numerous other young people who were in the same situation I was: unfulfilled at work, unwilling to settle for mediocrity, interested in making an impact, and trying to figure out what to do next.

One of those people was Evan Walden. Evan was four years younger than me, and had graduated from the University of Vermont in 2009 with a business degree. Interested in joining a start-up but pressured by the fear of post-graduate unemployment during a recession, he decided to take the best job he could find at the largest company that was offering the biggest paycheck. For two years, he sold pesticides for Dow Chemical, covering a $3.5 million territory and overseeing 80 distributor sales representatives.

Despite the recession, Evan went up 30% on his sales quotas and received a raise. He was good at selling chemicals, except there was one small problem: he wasn't *interested* in selling chemicals.

Evan says, "When I started at Dow, I experienced a few major things that I found deeply meaningful: living in California for the first time, being able to afford my own place, learning new skills, and being intentionally mentored by someone I admired. But I soon realized I wasn't building networks in the areas that I was most passionate about. The sales skills I was learning were invaluable, but the content of the job was hard for me to relate to. I felt out of place. I was missing a connection to the actual content of my work. Some people say that achieving the mastery of a skill breeds passion, and I think that's true, but when you become good at something, there's a desire to use that talent to affect a system that's bigger than yourself."

Evan's light went off in the summer of 2011, when he visited The Unreasonable Institute, a start-up accelerator program for impact-driven companies in Boulder, Colorado. There, his best friend from college Nathaniel was launching ReWork, a company to help people find fulfilling work with social enterprises and non-profits. When Evan felt himself light up around people who were working with purpose, he knew he was done selling chemicals.

"The day after I returned to California, I looked at myself in the mirror," Evan explains. "I tried to stare as deeply into my own eyes as I possibly could. A familiar feeling of fear washed over me. I felt guilty for wanting to walk away from my commitment. I was uncertain of how I'd pay the bills. But this decision was too important to be made out of fear. I was making this decision out of love. I walked over to the cabinet, took a shot of whiskey, and called my boss. I quit my job and never looked back."[21] Evan moved to Boulder, joining Nathaniel as a co-founder of ReWork.

One evening during StartingBloc, Evan and I were sitting at the rooftop bar of the Shangri-La Hotel, high above Santa Monica's palm trees. We sipped beers and watched the sun set over the Pacific Ocean. After I explained to him my dilemma of feeling stuck in a job that everyone else but me seemed to admire, he asked me one question: "Smiley, are you maximizing your potential?"

"No," I answered without hesitating. "I'm not fully engaged with my work, I'm not present. I want to be somewhere else."

"Why would you be doing anything less than maximizing your potential in life?" Evan asked me. The question hit me like a brick in the head. And at that moment, as the final waves of the day crested and broke under a purple-orange sky, I took a swig of beer, and hoisted my hands into the air like I had won an Olympic goal medal. I knew I had to quit my job, and more importantly, I knew that *I was going to quit my job.*

To be clear: I still had no idea what I was going to do next (this was still more than six months before I moved from D.C. to San Francisco). But I knew then that my breakthrough had begun. That was the first time, after feeling stuck for at least a year, that I felt empowered to make a change. Not once after that moment did I ever feel my Morning Edition, that brutal pain shooting up and down my spine.

The most significant moment of a breakthrough is beginning to listen to the voice within.

REMEMBER

If you want to turn your quarter-life crisis into a breakthrough and move beyond feeling stuck, hopeless, and FOMO'dosed, take tangible steps to explore what you're interested in. (In later chapters, we'll talk more about what those steps can look like). Express gratitude for the people in your life. Resist what can be so tempting—to compare yourself to others—and listen to the voice within, the one that's telling you to make a change.

Embracing the journey is not easy, quick, or simple. As soon as my light went off on that rooftop, I became scared of embarking on a completely new, uncertain career path at the ripe age of 28. But instead of making decisions out of fear, I focused on making decisions out of love, like Evan did. In the next chapter, we'll learn how to overcome fear by embracing it to guide our journey.

EMBRACING FEAR

Two weeks after StartingBloc, when I had that invincible feeling that I could do anything, Evan called me to check in while I was at work in Washington, D.C. "Did you have 'the talk' with your boss yet?" he asked me.

"No," I admitted.

"Why not?" he pressed.

"I don't know, I'll do it soon. This isn't a good month."

"*Smiley...*" he said, skeptically. What do you mean this isn't a good month?"

"Well, I'm scared," I said. "My boss told me I'm doing a great job and that I might get a raise soon, and my roommate told me to wait for my matching 401(k) plan to kick in next year, and then I could have non-competitive eligibility, a huge asset for federal employees."

"Whoa, wait a second," Evan fired back at me. "You told me you didn't want to stay in D.C., or work for the government anymore—you told me you were ready to leap now."

"I am ready to leap now," I said.

"So…what the hell are you waiting for?" asked Evan.

The truth was that I wasn't scared about leaving my job—I was terrified. Even though I knew I was ready to quit, the fear of leaping into a new career path at the age of 28 nearly crippled me. Even though I had determined that the most important thing to me was finding fulfilling work, I *still* felt pressured to play it safe.

Fear is a powerful force that can derail people's hopes and dreams. The journey requires *courage*—no one said it was going to be easy. If fear had gotten the best of us, you wouldn't be reading this book right now, Alex would have never registered 25,000 new voters, and Evan would still be selling chemicals somewhere in southern California.

During my quarter-life breakthrough, there were four fears I learned to embrace to help guide me to my next lily pad: *fear of the unknown, fear of failure, fear of what others will think,* and *fear of too many options.* This chapter will teach you how not to run from these fears, but use them as a source of positive energy and motivation.

Fear of the unknown → FEAR IS A SIGN

One of my mentors is 23 year-old Ted Gonder. You may think it's odd for someone who is 30 to have a mentor who is seven years younger, but that's because you haven't met Ted, an all-around badass. When Ted was in high school, he was interested in starting a small climate change awareness club. Someone told him he should turn the club into a national movement and call Bill Clinton and Al Gore to get their support. Ted thought the guy was nuts, but he made the call anyway. On the first couple calls, he got nothing but an answering machine. After a couple of tries, he eventually received a call back from Al Gore's COO, asking him to join The Climate Project as the student advisor and to help launch a network of climate change awareness clubs in public schools across the country. Ted has been embracing fear ever since those first phone calls.

In 2009, in the wake of the country's economic collapse, Ted co-founded Moneythink, a Chicago-based non-profit that teaches financial skills and entrepreneurial thinking to urban high school students. As someone who grew up with a lot of privilege, he became inspired to teach young people with less access how to manage their money, avoid debt, and start businesses. He's currently Moneythink's CEO and recently advised (yes, advised!) the Department of Homeland Security on ways to increase opportunities for immigrant entrepreneurs to come to the United States to work.

Ted gives an inspiring talk to young entrepreneurs called "Smashing Fear," which I've seen three times. During the talk, he shows YouTube videos of the fearless honey badger (motherfucker can run backwards!) sticking his head into a swarming beehive to extract the larvae. He also talks about his personal credo, one all of us can aspire to: fear is a tool, fear is fuel, fear is to be partnered with, we can listen to our fears to point us in the direction we need to walk. Ted says, "If we think of fear as an accomplice rather than an enemy, then we can be free to lean into it, and pursue our dreams, ideas, and projects freely."

In order to demonstrate the principle that anyone with courage can become an official fear-smasher, Ted hands out limes to everyone in the audience at the end of the talk. He asks everyone to bite into a whole lime to suck all the juice out (don't eat the peel!). It's hard to replicate this activity, but there's an energy in the room when everyone is chomping into limes and hurling the skins to the ground.

Rather than a sign of encouragement or motivation, fear all too often becomes a red light that puts the brakes on the very ideas, goals, and journeys that are right for us. Try shifting your perspective to view fear as a green light, an indicator that you're moving in the right direction.

BREAKTHROUGH EXERCISE

Fear Is A Sign

Write down one thing you're scared of doing (like quitting your job, launching a project, or moving to a new city). Ask yourself: why are you scared of doing this? Why does it frighten you? Is it scary because it's what you know you need to do?

Fear of failure → LEAN INTO FEAR

I recently ran a leadership development program in San Francisco called The Bold Academy, which brought together high-potential millennials interested in making career transitions. During Bold, participants are encouraged to lean into fear in order to explore which lily pad to leap to next. In order to demonstrate this principle, we divided our group into four teams, who all competed in what we called the "Bold Hustle," a 24-hour challenge to see which team could impact the most people without spending any money.

The winning team came up with the "Love Your Fear Project." Their idea was to ask people one simple question: If you could overcome any fear in the next six months, what would it be? They went to an art shop, convinced the manager to give them a 500-foot roll of construction paper (for free), got a taxi driver to drive them downtown (for free), and laid the paper outside the city's Ferry Building. Before they started, they nearly flinched. They got nervous that no one would write anything down and were scared their idea wouldn't work.

They began by writing their own fears down. Slowly, people started coming up to them, asking what they were doing. A woman who was afraid of heights wrote that she wanted to walk across the Golden Gate Bridge. Another man said he was afraid of being his own ethnicity in San Francisco. Another said he was afraid his business would fail. Another said he was afraid of raising his kids. Runners took a break to jot down their fears. The prime minister of Wales even walked by with his entourage and shared his fear.

After only four hours, 435 strangers had written their fears down on the roll of paper. Twice, the team had to convince the Department of Homeland Security that they weren't engaged in an act of terrorism (apparently it's illegal to talk about fear at a port).

The Love Your Fear Project demonstrated two things. First, fear is universal. Second, failure is impossible because by trying, you learn something. As one of the team members explained, "At the end of that day, our team felt so accomplished by what we'd just done, in embracing our own fears, that it didn't matter if we won the challenge. We ended up just doing that project for ourselves, which was overwhelmingly gratifying."

If you try something and it doesn't work out, so what? A powerful exercise is to ask yourself: what's the worst that could happen? I asked myself that when I weighed the decision whether to quit my job and this is what I wrote in my journal:

What's the worst that could happen? I quit, spend six months writing, and I can't find a new job. Worse case scenario, I go back to the job I left, which was still a good job at a great organization. And hey, at least I will have spent time exploring my interests, getting closer to what I want to do for the world, which is infinitely more valuable than staying at a job I don't like, so I can make a few thousand dollars.

When I asked myself what's the worst that could

happen when I thought about whether or not to write this book, this is what I wrote:

What's the worst that could happen? The book sucks, and the only person who reads it is my mom. But even if that's the case, I'll still have spent time learning how to express my ideas and tell a story, which is essential practice for a writer. At the very least, the process of writing a book will teach me something valuable.

Conversely, it's also worth asking yourself: what's the best-case scenario? What amazing, life-changing things could happen if you dream big and take a risk? What future could you create for yourself and for others? Use your imagination as you think of the most positive things that could happen. It might surprise you.

BREAKTHROUGH EXERCISE

Best-Case Scenario

Take what you were scared of doing from the previous exercise. As yourself: what's the worst that could happen if I pursue it? Even if you "fail" in this endeavor, how would you also be succeeding?

Now, ask yourself: what's the best that could happen if I pursue it?

Fear of what others will think ➔ WHOSE VOICE IS THIS?

Remember Alex, who left his job writing about the Boston Red Sox, despite the fact that a lot his friends (especially me) thought it was the coolest job ever? Or Kristen, who was ready to leave her job at Google, but was scared to make the leap for an entire year, feeling guilty because all her friends wanted to work there?

I had a very similar experience. I knew I was ready to leave my job at the Peace Corps, and as soon as I was getting excited about my plan to become a freelance writer, my parents, my boss, my co-workers, and even my close friends started telling me what a great job I had.

I had all these voices in my head telling me things like: "play it safe," "think about your 401(k) plan," "you're so good at your job," "quitting is going to affect your resume," "you have a great job—think about all the people who have master's degrees who would kill for your job."

These voices are incredibly powerful and they can sojourn a breakthrough. To ensure this doesn't happen, it's important to differentiate between which of these fears are actually *yours* and which of them are merely voices in your head from all the conversations you have every day with *other people*.

When I did this exercise, I realized that one of the fears preventing me from leaving my job was a recurring voice in my head that wasn't my own, rather it was the voice of several *co-workers* telling me I had a great job.

I asked myself: why would my co-workers ever tell me to leave my job if they liked working with me so much? I decided to *listen to the voice within,* take away all the advice everyone else had given me, and make the decision that was right for me. I also decided to *stop comparing myself to others* and remember that it doesn't matter what other people think. All that matters is that I know I'm ready to explore other interests.

An important caveat: it's not that your colleagues, parents, boss, and friends don't love you or that their advice is necessarily bad advice. They do love you and their advice might be perfectly sound. But people usually give advice that reflects their own experiences. Your co-worker, who has stayed in the same job for ten years, is probably not going to tell you to quit your job after two years. Someone like me, who recently quit my job to pursue my dream, is probably not going to tell you to stay in the same job for ten years if you're unhappy.

Your parents, who love you more than the world and want what's *safe* for you, might not know what's *right* for you. Your family, co-workers, friends, and even the author of this book all want to help you. But at the end of the day, the journey is personal: you're the only one that knows what's right for you. There's a *Seinfeld* episode where George Costanza claims he invented the "it's not you, it's me" routine. Get in the habit of saying, "it's not you, it's me."

Even people you look up to, even people who work in a career field you're interested in can give advice that's not right for you. Last spring, before I left my job at the Peace

Corps, I had coffee with one of my favorite journalists, an award–winning staff writer for *The New Yorker*. I told her I was thinking of leaving my job to start writing about subjects I was really interested in, and you know what she told me? "Don't quit your day job." Even though I completely respect her and her work, I chose to ignore her advice and listen to the voice within, remembering, "it's not you, it's me."

BREAKTHROUGH EXERCISE

The Voices

List all the doubts you currently have about your breakthrough. Now, determine the source of each of your doubts. Which are actually your own doubts? Which are coming from another source, like your parents, boss, co-workers, friends, or society?

Fear of too many options ➔ EVALUATE EACH AND DETERMINE WHICH FITS

Do you have trouble focusing or making decisions? Me too. I think every person born after 1980 has trouble focusing and making decisions. I can go from writing a sentence of this book, to checking my email to checking Facebook, to texting my friend to see if she wants to meet up later for a drink to eating some almonds to reading the *Buzzfeed* article my friend just posted to checking the homepage of *The New York Times*, all within 45 seconds.

The problem is that sometimes we act like this when it comes to major life decisions and it paralyzes us. When I first was thinking about my breakthrough, I was all over the place. I considered becoming an English teacher, a freelance writer, and working at a non-profit that produces documentaries.

I was too afraid to make the make wrong decision, so I made no decision at all. Fear of too many options kept me stuck. It's a fact of life that there are always two or more options and you could always be somewhere else. A good way to begin figuring out which option is the right fit for you is to take concrete steps towards determining which fits you best. Take a class in something you're interested in learning more about, read industry books and blogs, and talk to people working in areas you care about. Recall that Kristen was interested in a number of things other than becoming an esthetician. By signing up for an esthetics class, she discovered that doing make-up was something she wanted to pursue more seriously. Had she taken the class and not found it inspiring, she could cross it off the list and move onto something else.

In the next chapter, we'll discuss how you can avoid being stuck by trying many opportunities that interest you in the form of apprenticeships, internships, volunteering, consultancies, and short-term projects. This way, you can evaluate whether something is a fit in a shorter period of time.

We'll also discuss how to determine whether an opportunity is financially viable for you.

Every time you leap to another lily pad, you get a little bit closer to what you're looking for. I never would have done StartingBloc, moved to San Francisco, worked for The Bold Academy, started a blog, got published, or wrote this book if it hadn't been for my job at the Peace Corps—which might make it the most *meaningful* job I've ever had, precisely because it pushed me closer to realizing who I am and what I *actually* wanted to do.

REMEMBER

Fear is a powerful force that can derail a breakthrough. Fear is universal and avoiding it is futile. To get where you need to go, embrace fear to guide your journey instead of fighting it. Use fear as an indicator that you're on the right path. As Ted says, "If I'm not afraid to do something, it's probably not worth my time." Use fear to help you determine what your true voice within is telling you to do.

After my conversation with Evan on that rooftop in Santa Monica, I knew I had to make a change in my life. I knew I had to embrace fear and quit my job, despite the fact that everyone else in my life thought my job was awesome.

But I still had no idea what I was going to do next, not to mention how I would make my leap meaningful. However, unlike the previous year when I felt stuck and hopeless, I finally felt confident in my ability to explore what I wanted for the world after meeting other people who had already been through what I was experiencing.

In Part II, you'll get closer to how you can work with purpose by asking crucial questions that society has failed to ask since you were a little kid. First, you'll create your own definition of meaningful work, distinct from anyone else's. Then you'll align your definition with your job search. You'll learn techniques for finding new opportunities in a volatile job market, when to quit a job that's not the right fit, and realizing whether grad school makes sense for you.

BREAKTHROUGH EXERCISE

A Dancing Timeout

Whenever I'm about to do something important, like go to a job interview or present a project, I take a dancing timeout to shake out my stress and harness my energy. So go over to your stereo, or put on your headphones if you're in a public place (people may totally freak out, which is awesome), and blast your favorite song to dance to. My personal favorite is Robyn's "Dancing On My Own," but dance to whatever suits you.

PART II
ON FINDING
MEANINGFUL WORK

"How we spend our days is, of course, how we spend our lives."
-Annie Dillard

DISCOVERING MEANING

Evan asked me a question on that rooftop in Santa Monica that stayed with me ever since: "Why would you be doing anything less than maximizing your full potential in life?"

People maximize their potential when they work towards something greater than themselves and when they align their work with their purpose. Another way to think of your **purpose** is *what you want to do for the world*. When people reach their full potential, they change the world because they know *why* they're doing what they're doing. In my case, my current purpose is to help others reach their full potential through storytelling and creating transformative experiences like The Bold Academy.

Recall our definition of meaningful work from the introduction: **Meaningful work** provides personal meaning, reflecting **who you are** and **what your interests are**, allows you to **share your gifts** to **help others**, and is **financially viable** given your **desired lifestyle**.

A lot of books about finding meaningful work ask you to determine your calling in life. Those books scare the shit out of me. In this chapter we're simply going to ask the right questions to figure out *what your purpose is now*, so you can figure out which lily pad to leap to next.

Let's accept the idea that very few people have only one purpose, one truth, or one calling. Our purpose actually changes throughout our lives as we try different jobs, travel to new places, meet new people, and grow older. Over the last 30 years, I've had numerous different "callings," from being Big Bird to being a sports writer to making movies—and I'm currently doing none of those things.

We each have to define meaning for ourselves and accept that our definition might change over time. For example, Alex found meaning over several years from writing about baseball, registering people to vote, and tweeting for the U.S. Ambassador to the United Nations.

In this chapter, we'll break down our definition of meaningful work into five components, and ask a few basic questions that will lead to complex answers. Your responses will get you closer to realizing how you can maximize your potential by aligning your work with your purpose.

Defining Meaningful Work

1. Meaningful work reflects who you are

While I was at StartingBloc, it was daunting to realize that I was 28 years old and I *still* hadn't figured out who I was. Sure, on paper, I had *everything* figured out: I had a job, a nice apartment, great benefits, and girls (occasionally) would go out with me. But the truth was that I hadn't yet discovered *why I was here.*

To try and figure out my purpose during my breakthrough, I read *What Color is Your Parachute?* (for the second time), took a Myers-Briggs personality test and completed StrengthsFinder, did lots of yoga, and contemplated going on a pilgrimage to a temple somewhere in Asia, but decided that buying a $1500 plane ticket would be unwise, given the fact that I was going to quit my job in a few months.

While all of these tools can be helpful, it turns out that the most useful thing I did cost no money at all. I broke out my Moleskine journal and wrote down the answers to a series of self-discovery questions, which I've included in the upcoming exercises. If these questions seem rudimentary, that's because they are. However, many people go much of their adult lives without ever asking themselves these questions, which might explain why 70% of the U.S. population spend their days not engaged at work.

"What's the first thing people notice about you?" is one of the questions that you are encouraged to answer when setting up your online dating profile on OkCupid. I prefer the related but more relevant question: *what do you love about yourself?*

When I first asked myself this question, I answered as if I were in a job interview. I assumed my greatest asset was my hard work ethic and my ability to multitask. After some reflection, I realized that what I love about myself actually has nothing to do with the workplace whatsoever. What I love about myself is my ability to laugh and smile despite all the trouble in the world and stress in my life. I think I inherited this attitude of "it could always be worse," from my grandparents, who lost everything in the Depression, and faced problems a lot more serious than having Facebook-induced FOMO.

When I say that I smile a lot, it might be an understatement. I got the nickname "Smiley" my second week of high school. I wanted to play a sport. I wasn't good enough to make the soccer team. Football was out of the question since I was about five feet tall and 110 pounds. I wasn't coordinated enough to do crew. The only other option was cross country. So I went to practice. I didn't even know what cross country was, and I looked at the coach like he was nuts when he told us to go run five miles along the Charles River.

"Wait, we just go running?" I asked.

"Yes, kid, we run, that's what we do, what did you think this was?" he said.

"I actually have no idea," I replied. "It sounded fun."

My coach, an All-American runner in high school, was also from Cambridge. One chilly day, we were running a hill workout, which involved running up and down a huge hill, over and over again. About fourteen hills in, exhausted, I was nearing the top of the hill, digging in and struggling with a big grin on my face. "What the fuck-aah-ya-doin' smilin' kid?!" my coach screamed at me in his thick Boston accent. "Yaaah not supposed to be smilin', yaaah supposed to be pukin', staaaup smilin', staaaht pukin', staaaht pukin' kid!''

From then on, the team called me Smiley. This is a core piece of my personality that needs to be present in my day-to-day. I don't want to feel like I need to put on an "act" at the office, or try to be someone I'm not. I want to be able to show up every day as myself, unwavering smile and all.

BREAKTHROUGH REFLECTION

Where Your Heart Resides

Try answering as many of these questions as you can, writing without stopping as you move through each question. Don't judge the answer, just write what comes to mind. If you prefer to just reflect on them, that's okay too. Do what works for you.

- What do you love about yourself?

- How are you different from your friends?

- What makes you, *you*?

- What makes you weird? (Being weird is good.)

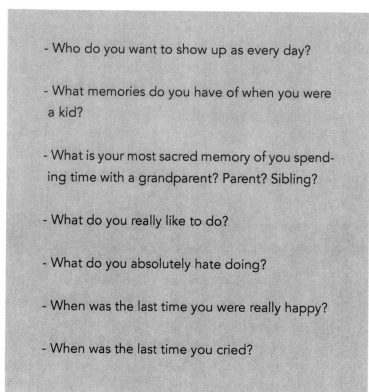

- Who do you want to show up as every day?

- What memories do you have of when you were a kid?

- What is your most sacred memory of you spending time with a grandparent? Parent? Sibling?

- What do you really like to do?

- What do you absolutely hate doing?

- When was the last time you were really happy?

- When was the last time you cried?

2. Meaningful work reflects your interests

We have to figure out for ourselves what we care most about, and these interests often evolve. Alex grew up a self-proclaimed, die-hard baseball nerd, but was drawn to volunteer for Obama's presidential campaign in 2008 because of his changing interests. The reason I wanted to work at the Peace Corps was because the job deeply aligned with issues I cared about. I believed in Peace

Corps' mission to promote world peace and friendship, and I believed in the work 8,000 Peace Corps volunteers were doing in remote communities all over the world.

Sometimes we don't have to look too far to find the personal experience that shapes our interests, and how to incorporate our interests into our work. Tom D'Eri, 24, had been interested in social innovation and sustainable business since early on in college at Bentley University. Upon graduation, he considered positions in corporate social responsibility, but the corporate world didn't move him. Instead, he went back to an idea he had in college that was inspired by his brother Andrew, who has autism.

Although his brother is a vibrant young man, Tom saw his brother's disability put him at a clear disadvantage when it came to securing meaningful employment. So alongside his father, Tom built Rising Tide Car Wash in south Florida, which employs and empowers people with autism. The family business provides people of all ability levels an opportunity to build a career and an independent life.

Tom explained to me that his company provides meaning to his employees because for the first time in many of their lives, they have an opportunity to provide something valuable to others. They also get to be part of a community that celebrates what makes them unique. "As novel as a job at a car wash may be to the average person," Tom explains, "we're seeing tremendous improvement in our employees' self-esteem and social skills." Rising Tide also provides meaning to its customers because they can vote with their dollar, making the business case for employing individuals with disabilities.

We often think of interests as academic subjects like art, history, or science. But interests are really anything that energizes you. For Tom, that meant his own family and the challenges facing people with disabilities that he had seen first-hand. By picking a cause near to his heart, Tom embarked on a journey to build a business that provides personal meaning to him, as well as meaning to his employees and customers.

BREAKTHROUGH REFLECTION

What Moves You

Reflect on the following questions, either in writing or aloud:

- What do you care about?

- What gets you fired up?

- What happened that made you change the way you see the world?

- What personal life experiences have shaped your beliefs?

- What injustice infuriates you?

- What types of articles do you find yourself posting on Facebook?

- What social issues are you most passionate about?

If you're having trouble determining what moves you, browse a newspaper or magazine and notice which articles you're drawn to reading.

3. Meaningful work allows you to share your gifts

A lot of inspirational blogs simply tell you to "follow your passion!" It's like, *"No shit, if I knew what my one passion was, I wouldn't be reading your blog."* From my experience, it's far easier to find meaningful work if you use your unique gifts (your strengths and skills) as your calling card alongside your interests, rather than your passion (or in my case, my 11 passions).

For example, I'm deeply passionate about making others laugh. I smile so often that whenever I'm at a bar, bulky dudes with tattoos and baseball caps look at me like they're about to pound my face into the Big Buck Hunter arcade machine. I love Larry David and Dave Chappelle but this doesn't mean I want to work as a stand-up comedian.

Instead, I want work that allows me to share my gifts with the world: writing, spreading positive energy, interacting with people, and creating transformative experiences that help purpose-driven leaders.

Many people who find their work fulfilling have achieved some degree of expertise in their work. It feels great to be good at something. Skills often get people hired and they usually determine what you'll be doing for eight to ten hours a day.

Skills can also provide leverage and allow you to take your career in multiple directions, which is ever more important in an unstable job market. Alex was able to utilize his writing and communications skills to pursue a range of opportunities in sports journalism, government, and the technology sector.

If you want to read more about why skills matter, check out Cal Newport's excellent book *So Good They Can't Ignore You: Why Skills Trump Passion in the Quest for Work You Love*, or Daniel Pink's *Drive: The Surprising Truth About What Motivates Us*.

If you're good at something you don't like doing, find something else to be good at

When I worked at the Peace Corps, I spent the majority of my days doing administrative tasks: scheduling meetings and conference calls, compiling to-do lists, drafting memos, and planning events, to name a few. I happen to be very good at detail-oriented administrative work—years of neuroses have made me a meticulous planner. Sometimes I even write to-do lists of things I've *already done*, because it makes me feel good to cross them off. My boss and my teammates loved working with me because I used to keep us all on task and goal-oriented.

The only problem was that I didn't actually *like* doing detail-oriented administrative work. I hated scheduling meetings, making agendas, and trying to get memos approved in a bureaucracy. I wanted to do more writing and creative projects. It's nice to know that I have a practical skill if I ever need a job in the future doing project management, administrative work, or event planning, but it's also important to recognize when something you're good at is not the right fit. In the end, it wasn't that I didn't enjoy working at the Peace Corps—an incredible organization full of brilliant colleagues that aligned with my interests—it's that I didn't enjoy what I was doing every day from 9-to-5 (or more like 8-to-8).

Being good at something can get you a great job. However, having a skill you're good at but that you hate doing may keep you from finding meaningful work. In the next exercise, you'll differentiate between things you're good at that make you miserable and things you're good at that you love.[22]

If you need to develop a new skill, start learning now

A lot of people only pursue things they're naturally good at, which is fine if you want to be a playwright and you've been writing plays since the second grade. But it was problematic for someone like me, who decided he wanted to start writing after not taking a single English class in college and spending his first seven years after graduation working in film and politics. If you want to pursue something you don't know much about or something you're not very good at, *admit what you don't know and take steps immediately towards learning more and improving that skill.*

At the age of 28, when I decided I wanted to pursue writing, I hadn't published anything besides articles for my high school and college newspapers. While still working at the Peace Corps, I started having coffee with every single writer I knew to ask how they got started and how they practiced writing. I read books on writing like Anne Lamott's *Bird by Bird*, Julia Cameron's *The Artist's Way*, and Steven Pressfield's *The War of Art*. Most importantly, I followed my freelance-writer-friend Ryan's advice and took a small step: I created a blog and started writing regularly.

When my friend Zack Shapiro, now 24, graduated from the University of Colorado–Boulder, he was interested in joining a tech start-up. But he soon realized that most of the tech jobs were for programmers. Zack didn't know much about coding, since he majored in media studies in college and spent his free time getting people on campus excited about the college basketball team.

Because he knew he needed to develop his skills in order to work at a start-up, he taught himself how to code. He bought *The Rails Tutorial,* an introduction to a coding framework, and practiced using the exercises in the book.

When Zack met the Vice President of Engineering of tech start-up TaskRabbit at the South by Southwest Conference, he pitched him on an internship even though he was still learning how to code. He got the part-time internship and gained expertise from working around programming experts at TaskRabbit. The internship eventually turned into a paid, full-time job.

Zack quickly built up his coding skills. Interested in giving people control of their social networks, he began building his own app on nights and weekends. His app Silencer mutes spoilers, people, hashtags, and terms on Twitter and Facebook so people can avoid knowing what happened in the *Game of Thrones* episode they missed, but all their friends saw.

Silencer has been downloaded more than 10,000 times and has been featured in *Lifehacker, Fast Company*, and *CNET.* These days, Zack is hard at work on creating another innovative business app called Luna, a nighttime delivery service for the city of San Francisco. He's reaching his potential because he got the skills he needed to make his ideas come to life, not because he was passionate about start-ups.

It's intimidating to begin learning a new skill like Zack did with programming or I did with writing. Be okay with being a beginner. Everyone has to start somewhere.

BREAKTHROUGH REFLECTION

Discovering Your Gifts

Make a list of *everything* you're good at, including things like baking and breakdancing, not only resume skills like Microsoft Excel and grant writing. Think about things you were really good at as a kid, in high school, and during college. These are your unique skills and strengths, your gifts to the world.

Now, cross off the things on this list that you don't actually *like* doing. What areas do you need to deepen your knowledge in? What types of classes do you need to take? What books do you need to read? What experts do you need to talk to?

Pick one thing on that list you need to deepen your knowledge of or start learning about—and then explore concrete ways to improve that skill.

4. Meaningful work allows you to help others

Now, it's time to bring the pieces of your meaningful work definition together: what holds your personality, your interests, and your gifts in place is *how* you're going to help others. By this I mean, determining *what type of impact* you want to make.

Although there are infinite ways people can make an impact with their work, I find it helpful to ask a few questions: *Do I need to see the results of my work every single day? Do I need to have a face-to-face relationship with the people I'm serving, or can I make an indirect impact behind the scenes?*

Face-to-face impact implies that you're working with the person you're helping on a daily basis, allowing you to see the purpose of your work up close. Think of people on the front lines: a classroom teacher, an aid worker, a community organizer, a coach, or a doctor.

You can also make an indirect impact. You may not see your impact on a daily basis, but you know that over time, your work is contributing towards a cause greater than yourself. There's an element of delayed gratification. Think of the people behind the scenes: a research scientist, a policy analyst, a programmer, or a consultant.

From my experience working at the Peace Corps, I learned that it was not enough for me to be working behind the scenes for administrators, drafting memos and enhancing agency policies in Washington, D.C., which impacted over 8,000 volunteers working in 75 countries. My experience taught me the valuable lesson that, personally, I would have been a lot more fulfilled working face-to-face with several villagers in rural Botswana than drafting memos in a cubicle in a 500-person office building in the nation's capital. Learning *how* you want to do your work is equally as valuable as learning *what* you want to do in the first place.

Gayle Abrams' journey to figure out how to share her gifts as an educator is a great example of this idea. One opportunity I explored during my breakthrough was teaching. Gayle, 27, has been a teacher for the past five years and invited me to visit her classroom.

"When you see a great teacher, you are seeing a work of art," said Geoffrey Canada, founder of the Harlem Children's Zone. When I first heard this quote, I immediately thought of Gayle. Gayle has the uncanny ability to light up a classroom, using games and jokes to get her 4th graders excited about learning. Thirty minutes into their geometry lesson, each of her students had demonstrated the difference between parallel, perpendicular, and intersecting lines, and were competing in a game to point out as many examples of each in the classroom—one kid even spotted perpendicular lines on my blue marine-themed socks.

Gayle loves both math and teaching—she once choreographed a dance with her class to Daft Punk's "Around The World," and then performed it with them in the school talent show. But her work nearly drove her to the point of burnout. As Gayle describes, "I was working as a math specialist in a high-need urban elementary school, teaching 4th grade math...I gave every bit of my being to teaching my 4th graders math conceptually, with the goal that they would succeed on the standardized assessment. And they did—with results that my school district had never seen before. The pressure I put on myself was worth it. But, the following year the pressure to maintain that level of success caused my eye to twitch for three months straight."

Gayle's personal life brought her to a new city, and she was hired as a 5th grade literacy teacher in a charter school that emphasizes innovation and caring for the environment over test scores. "I thought I found my cure," Gayle says. "But I was still struggling. I came home each night hanging by a thread. I felt like I was failing my students. I couldn't motivate and engage *all* of them. I couldn't make *all* of them proficient readers. People would tell me, 'You can't take this home with you. You can't save them all. You're an amazing teacher and your kids love you.' My identity had become so wrapped up in my work. I knew the only way I could fully gain any sense of clarity was to take a step back."

Listening to the voice within, Gayle explored options in math education outside of the classroom. Feeling drained (understandably so—Gayle treats math class like others treat Zumba), Gayle sought out and accepted opportunities to be both an instructional coach for teachers at her school and a math education consultant for a national company. In these roles, she works to improve the quality of math education throughout the country.

Instead of merely having an impact on her classroom

of 25 students, she's now working towards changing the way math teachers in schools across the country light up their classrooms. "Now I get to hear stories of other teachers and learn from their perspectives, so that maybe one day I'll be able to go back into the classroom with a sense of balance and resilience I was missing," says Gayle.

There are a variety of needs within any field or career, and the impact we want to make may be different at 25 and at 30. We need talented teachers in the classroom, talented people to train teachers, and talented people to set the policies and standards to ensure that what kids are actually learning will help them become engaged global citizens.

Gayle's story is one of *flexibility* and *experimentation*. By making a small pivot within her career, she found meaningful work. Gayle may find after a year or two that she prefers classroom teaching to education consulting. And that's perfectly okay, but how would she know that until she took a break from the classroom and tried something new?

The question for Gayle was not "Is it more impactful to be a classroom teacher, or an math education consultant?" Just like the question for Alex was not "Is it more impactful to write about baseball or register people to vote?" All of these options are impactful in one way or another—the goal is to determine whether an opportunity allows you to make the type of impact you want to make right now.

BREAKTHROUGH REFLECTION

Impact

Again, write answers to the following questions or reflect on them aloud:

- What type of impact do you want to have?

- What type of impact have you had in previous jobs?

- Do you need to see the results of your work every single day?

- Do you need to have a face-to-face relationship with the people you're serving?

5. Meaningful work is financially viable given your desired lifestyle

The final part of our meaningful work definition is finding work that is **financially viable** given your **desired lifestyle**. Many blog posts I read when I was thinking about quitting my job overlooked the small yet crucial detail of how the hell I was supposed to support myself once I leapt. They said, "just go for it, follow your passion, don't worry about money!" I thought, does this person want me to jump from a moving airplane? Are they fucking nuts?

That philosophy might work for early employees at Facebook, but I still owe Sallie Mae thousands of dollars in student loans, on top of rent, bills, and health care, so money is something I take very seriously. The advantage to worrying about money is that it made me a smart financial planner. I stayed in my job at least six months longer than I wanted to in order to save up enough money to avoid being a nervous wreck when I quit.

The downside of worrying about money is that it often keeps us from taking steps towards actually making money (finding a new job, starting a business, doing your work, selling your work). In the amount of time I've complained over the past year about how hard it is to get paid well for freelance pieces, I probably could have written a second book.

Whether you're self-employed or working for another organization (especially in an entry-level position), you may have to have multiple jobs and find more than one source of income to support yourself. In case you haven't checked your news feed recently: shit is rough out there.

Shit is especially rough for writers. My friend Ryan, the freelance journalist who often writes for *The New York Times*, has adapted to the changing economy. He says, "As for being an independent journalist, it's important in your early years to stay above water. You learn to live on less than most people; for me, I threw away the things that I couldn't afford any more (eating at restaurants regularly, going to bars all the time). A lot of people take jobs outside the world of journalism to make money—such as tutoring, bartending, or waiting tables—while reporting the heck out of some quality stories. In my early years of freelancing, I supplemented my income by tutoring high school students in writing, and also moonlighting a few nights a week as a referee for a young professionals dodgeball league."

"It was a grind, and often wore me down, but after a few years of writing quality stories and acquiring more and more assignments, I was able to drop those side gigs and focus all my energy on writing. Furthermore, I see my occupation as that of storyteller, and this opens me up to other non-print assignments—like television and film, both areas I've also worked in. You have to be flexible and also curious enough to try various assignments."

In between pitching stories to publications like *The New York Times*, *Men's Journal*, and *Deadspin*, Ryan has written copy for NBC's Olympics coverage, was an associate producer on ESPN's *30 for 30* documentary *Benji*, and worked on an Emmy award-winning story for HBO's *Real Sports with Bryant Gumbel* (as well as pay his bills)—all because he's remained flexible and been open to finding multiple income sources.

When you're considering new meaningful job opportunities, make sure that these positions provide you enough money to live the life you want to live. In order to keep his head above water as a freelance writer, Ryan was willing to make lifestyle sacrifices, like going out to dinner less often, that some people might not be willing to make. Remember that the journey is personal—we each have unique financial needs and responsibilities. Some of us have enormous student loans to pay off or health concerns. Some of us have children and some of us are taking care of families.

A good way to determine the cost of your desired lifestyle is to consider your estimated weekly and monthly expenses. This may include things like food, transportation, rent, utilities, and entertainment. Factor in loan payments, healthcare, and other bills you might have. Think about how much money you'd like to save each month for the future.

You might want to conduct a personal finance audit and start keeping a budget. There are free websites that help you track your expenses (like Mint.com) and others that provide more in–depth financial planning advice for a small cost (like LearnVest). See the Resources section for more, and consider talking to an accountant and/or personal finance advisor if you're struggling with this.

Balancing Money and Meaning

In my experience, finding meaningful work is a never-ending balancing act. You have to balance each of these five components, and determine what your breakthrough priorities are. Your **breakthrough priority** is your bottom line which says: *above all else, even if I have to make certain sacrifices, it's most important that the next lily pad I jump to allows me to _____.*

Is it more important to you that you get a job in your dream city or at your target organization? Is it more important that you're developing new skills or that you have a lot of autonomy at work? Is it more important that you do work you truly care about or make a lot of money?

I made about half as much money this past year as the previous one, but my life was about ten times more meaningful because I was doing work that made me come alive and living in a city I loved. As we'll see in Chapters 5 and 6, I've found that pursuing a meaningful lifestyle is not about salary line as much as it is about living in alignment with your purpose and priorities and surrounding yourself with supportive communities.

The breakthrough priorities we set for ourselves and the choices we make at a young age matter. If Alex's breakthrough priority in 2008 had been job stability over joining Obama's presidential campaign, he would have missed out on an opportunity to change history. If you value a job so much that you don't move to a new city with your partner, you may lose the person you love. If you put money over meaning, you may end up rich but unfulfilled.

I'll never forget a conversation I had with one of my older colleagues at the Peace Corps, not long after I first started. My colleague had been with the organization for almost ten years, was a senior manager, and married with a family. I told her I didn't really like living in D.C.—the politics, the workaholics, and the humidity weren't for me—and that my dream since college was to live in San Francisco.

She told me that she and her husband had always wanted to leave D.C. when they were younger and move to a different place, but they got stuck because of her job. She mentioned that sometimes you have to make sacrifices in life, and that their priority had been job security over living in a place where they would have been more fulfilled. If she could do it all over again, she would have probably chosen fulfillment over job security, she told me. Her advice to me: based on my priorities, now was the time to take a risk; that the longer I stayed, the older I got, and the more life responsibilities I took on, the harder it was going to be to leave.

REMEMBER

To find meaningful work, you need to figure out the **why**: why you wake up in the morning and what you want to do for the world. Reaching your potential means aligning your work with your purpose.

In order to figure out what your purpose is now, examine your personality and your interests, how you want to share your gifts to help others, and what type of impact you want to make. In addition to being in line with this purpose, the lily pad you leap to next needs to provide enough money so that you can live a lifestyle that works for you. Very few people discover meaning overnight. Tom spent many years with his brother and father, before deciding to start a business with them. Zack spent months learning how to code before he could even work for a start-up, let alone build his own app. Gayle was working as a classroom teacher for five years before she leapt to a new lily pad to start consulting and mentoring other teachers.

The art of trying to align your work with your purpose and balance your priorities in a constantly changing job market in the midst of a global recession (where 25% of 25-34 year-olds aren't employed!) is by no means easy. At times, alignment can feel close to impossible. But in the next chapter, you'll learn how to beat the odds and make meaningful choices when it comes to putting your self-discovery work into practice during your job search.

ALIGNING YOUR GIFTS WITH YOUR IMPACT

Self-discovery is a crucial step in the journey, and the next steps deal with applying this reflection to your job search and getting a job in today's volatile job market.

This chapter will teach you how best to determine what meaningful work looks like to you by finding opportunities that match your values and allow you to share your gifts with the world. We'll go over a few easy ways to kick-start your meaningful job search and discuss when it makes sense to leave a position that's not working for you. And finally, we'll take a look at the question that has plagued me for the past ten years: is graduate school worth it?

Alignment

A lot of people spend years searching in vain for the "perfect job." Accept the possibility that the perfect job might not exist for everyone, or that the perfect job at the age of 22 is different than at the age of 28. Instead, adopt a new goal: *to find a job or opportunity, based on your purpose now, that allows you to share your gifts to make a positive impact in the lives of others.*

Instead of looking for the perfect job, start your meaningful job search where as many of your motivations overlap. Take your definition of meaningful work from the previous chapter, and turn it into an alignment Venn diagram showing **your gifts** (your personality, interests, and skills), the **impact** you want to have on the world, and your desired **quality of life**.

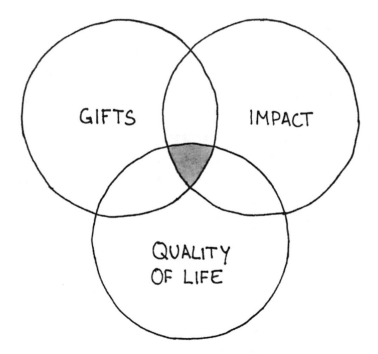

Months after hoisting my hands in the air overlooking the Pacific Ocean, I finally embraced my fears to have "the talk" with my boss about leaving my job at Peace Corps. Her response was that I should stay another year. Her rationale: employers really like to see that you worked for at least three years in every job.

While it's true that every employer wants to see a demonstrated track record of commitment (no manager wants to hire someone who's going to bail in six months)—I decided to leave after a little more than two years. My rationale: I had learned all I could in my current role in two years. During a third year, I would have only been passing the time so a hypothetical future employer may or may not have said, "Well, good thing you did three years at Peace Corps, you're hired."

Instead of making a decision based on a hypothetical unknown, I made a decision based on current known factors: my job was not in alignment with my *gifts*, the *impact* I wanted to make, or my desired *quality of life*. I knew what I didn't want: I didn't want a job that was administrative rather than creative, I didn't want to be making an indirect impact with my work, I didn't want to pretend to be someone I wasn't by working unhealthy hours in a large government bureaucracy, and I didn't want to live in Washington, D.C.

I found alignment from moving across the country and embarking on a completely new career path. When I got offered the job as the director of The Bold Academy, I knew it was the right fit for me because I could share my *gifts* to inspire others and show up every day as my positive, creative self. I knew I would be making the type of *impact* I wanted to make by encouraging others to reach their potential and supporting young entrepreneurs. And I knew that living with creative people in the Bay Area, prioritizing work–life balance, and having time to spend on my personal writing would support my desired *quality of life*.

As you begin your search for the next lily pad to leap to, look for positions where you can share your unique gifts at organizations that match your values and provide the opportunity to make an impact, and the quality of life you desire. In other words, find the sweet spot where as many of the pieces as possible overlap.

The alignment process—fitting these pieces together—often takes time and patience. I dislike delayed gratification as much as the next young person, but there's no easy button. Ryan, the journalist, has been freelancing for over eight years (and writing professionally for more than thirteen years). It wasn't until recently that he stopped refereeing dodgeball to help pay the bills.

Given the realities of the job market and your level of expertise, there may not be a position currently available that aligns exactly with what you're looking for or you may not be qualified for the position you want. Manage your expectations: if you're applying for your first job out of college or changing fields, you may not yet have the skills you need to get what you want. If that's the case, use the job searching tactics detailed later in this chapter to find a short-term apprenticeship or opportunity that will help you get closer to where you want to be in the future. Remember, a breakthrough isn't about finding the perfect alignment overnight. It's simply about *finding a job or opportunity, based on your current purpose that allows you to share your gifts and to make a positive impact in the lives of others.*

Here are several questions to ask when searching for meaningful work and determining alignment:

1. Do the organization's core values reflect my *purpose?* Does this position allow me to share my *gifts?*

2. Will I make the *type of impact* I want to make? (Think back to the example of Gayle leaving the classroom, but still continuing her work in education.)

3. Is the size of the organization, the work environment, and the culture the right fit for me?

4. Will this job allow me to be *fulfilled outside of work?* Will the salary and benefits support the quality of life I want for myself/my family? Will I have healthy work–life balance? How long is the commute? Do I have to move far away from my partner or my close friends? Do I want to live in the city where the job is?

Janet Frishberg's Journey to Alignment

Alignment can come from moving 3,000 miles across the country like I did, or it can come from finding a work-life balance and new colleagues that energize you. A year ago, Janet Frishberg, 25, was working for a workforce development non-profit in San Francisco, helping job seekers write cover letters, draft resumes, and prepare for interviews. Although the work reflected her values, she found herself drained and needing a break from the non-profit sector. As she remembers, "I was burnt out and ready for a change of pace and to learn about a new world outside of non-profits, which was where I'd been working for most of my professional life. I also noticed that I was having a lot of trouble with work-life boundaries; for instance, I'd go to sleep thinking about my clients and wake up thinking about them almost every day. This made it quite difficult to relax, and to focus on my life outside of work, which was really important to me. I never felt like I could do enough."

Janet decided to leap to another lily pad. She leveraged the job-placement skills she had gained from three years at the non-profit *(gifts),* and her interest in helping people find work *(impact)* with a job in technical recruiting at Airbnb. "I figured if I was changing sectors and industries, I might as well use some of the same skills so it'd be clear to employers how I'd be a fit," recalls Janet. "I was looking for a cohesive and collaborative team, a position where there'd be large opportunity for growth and professional development, and a company mission or product that I believed in. I wanted to feel like I could make a large impact but not be completely underwater every day, to find a company that viewed employees as humans rather than robots *(quality of life)."*

She found the transition to a completely new industry (tech) and a new sector (for-profit) invigorating. "I love my job at Airbnb," explains Janet. "Almost everything the company wants to do requires engineers, so it feels very relevant to be building out that team. I get a lot of gratification from the way we hire candidates. I believe in our process and enjoy helping people through the steps of evaluating whether this will be the best next move for them in their lives. Also, I adore my coworkers, both on my team and in the company in general. One thing I love is that most people have outside of work interests that are seen as strengthening (rather than threatening) to their primary jobs. I'm always learning from the people I work with."

Janet finds meaning in working alongside her colleagues at Airbnb. "We laugh a lot throughout the day," she says. "I get really silly sometimes. It's probably the most myself at work that I've ever felt in a professional setting, which isn't a coincidence. There's a team of people working to ensure that we maintain a culture of authenticity in our office. It's energizing to be part of this collaborative, supportive unit of people."

In addition to being a technical recruiting coordinator, Janet is an extremely talented writer. She's currently working on her first book, a memoir about grief that was sparked by the death of her good friend when she was 17. I first met Janet at a reading she gave for an anthology she had contributed to called *Get Out of My Crotch: Twenty-One Writers Respond to America's War on Women's Rights and*

Reproductive Health. I asked her why she didn't pursue her love for writing full-time and how she manages to find time to write her book with her 9-to-5 job.

"Right now, I'm a better artist when I know how I'm going to pay my rent and buy my bus pass and all that," Janet told me. "I also know some people who feel like better artists when their income is dependent on their art because it forces them into action, and maybe one day I'll feel like that. In terms of finding the time, there are 168 hours in a week. So let's say I spend 52 of those at work on an average week, and 56 of them sleeping. That still leaves me with something like 60 hours to write, if I want to. I don't have dependents, or many required responsibilities outside of work and taking care of myself, so I have a lot of privilege with how I choose to spend my time.

To make writing a priority, I'll stay in on weekend nights, which makes me feel kind of boring and also happy. I write on the bus in 10-minute segments. I do place a high precedence on my relationships, which are incredibly important to me. But, there are other activities I just don't do right now, things I know a lot of people enjoy. For instance, I don't watch TV or read magazines. Also, I used to drink a lot and when I started writing more, I stopped drinking as much because I was losing so much time to feeling not great the day after. These days, it's rare that I have more than one drink. I'm trying to figure out how to use the time in a way that reflects what I want to be building and creating right now, and also to not be too much of a perfectionist about what I do take on. I like waking up excited about each day."

Soon after this interview, Janet's schedule was thrown off-balance when she began a 9-month training program to become a counselor, and she acknowledges that she's still trying to find the space for everything in a given week. However, by being flexible and mindful of her time, Janet has been able to balance her work at Airbnb and nurture her writing, a task that eludes many writers I know. In pursuing alignment, she has found meaning, inside and outside of the workplace.

How to Kick-start Your Meaningful Job Search

Now that you have a better sense of what worked for Janet and how to align potential opportunities with your purpose, here are a few job search tactics that you can try out.

Signal the noise

Finding meaningful work requires going a step further than a normal job search. Sure, you need to do your usual homework: polish your resume, find companies and positions that interest you, and conduct informational interviews. But the truth is, searching for a meaningful job on your own is an exercise in futility.

Because the competition is stiff, you need to "signal the noise," as my friend Sydney Malawer, a human-centered design strategist for impact-driven companies says. Recruit a cadre of supporters to find openings that might be a good fit for you. The more closely aligned your supporters are with your values and what you're looking for, the more likely they'll be able to connect you with the right job leads.

Find meetups and groups of people doing the work you want to be doing. By sharing your story and what you're looking for with these groups, you'll increase your chances of reaching your goals. If you're having trouble identifying these groups, there are numerous organizations already on the lookout for meaningful jobs. Many organizations like ReWork, Echoing Green, Net Impact, and B Lab have a variety of resources available for job seekers, including job boards and regional networking events. Check the Resources section for more information.

Use other people's networks

My friend Jesse recently completed a master's degree in comparative religion, and is looking for jobs that further his goal of increasing inter-religious dialogue between Muslims and non-Muslims at home and abroad. Knowing that as many as 80% of jobs are not published, he reached out to everyone he knew.[23]

But after a couple of weeks, he realized that his contacts hadn't produced any substantial job leads. He tried a new approach: he made a list of people working at the organizations he was interested in working for, and worked backward to see if he could be connected to those people through friends of friends. He even hand-drew a visual chart of his networking web, so he could keep track of all the people he wanted to talk to. By reaching beyond his network (to other people's networks), Jesse lined up a slew of phone calls, informational interviews, and actual job interviews.

Regardless of whether you create a visual networking web or make a list of your job leads, the important thing is to not limit your search to people within your network. Use other people's networks to get closer to the folks you need to talk to.

Make the ask (even on a bicycle)

Several months ago, I was riding my bicycle through San Francisco's Mission district when a guy biked up next to me and started talking to me at a red light. He asked, "Hey, how was your day today, was it a hard day?"

I wondered, who's this crazy weirdo trying to talk to me? I ignored him, and as soon as the light turned green, I began biking faster, planning my escape route. The man started biking faster as well and kept talking to me. He told me his name was Bernat Fortet Unanue, and he had recently moved to San Francisco from Barcelona. Coincidentally, I had just returned from a vacation to Barcelona, visiting my best friend who lived in the neighborhood where Bernat grew up.

We kept biking together for another fifteen minutes and talking. Bernat told me he had been job hunting for over a month with no luck. He explained that he was a

user experience and user interface (UX/UI) designer—
one of the best in Barcelona—and was on his way home
from his third job interview of the day. He was desperately
trying to find a job in San Francisco. He asked me what
I was up to, and I told him that I was writing a book for
people looking for meaningful work.

He said, "Do you have a cover designer yet?"

"No," I said. "Actually, I've been looking for one."

Bernat gave me his website, and when I got home, I
checked it out. His work was amazing. We met again for
tacos later that week, and I asked Bernat to design the
cover of my book. He said, "Of course!"

Knowing Bernat was still looking for work, I posted a
link to Bernat's website on my Facebook wall, saying, "If
anyone in the Bay Area is looking for an incredible UX/
UI designer, you should talk to my buddy Bernat, he hails
from Barcelona—and his work is incredible."

My friend Yee saw my Facebook post and emailed Bernat, telling him about an opportunity to work as the lead
designer for his friend's innovative mobile software start-up
in Palo Alto, California. Bernat met with the team that week
and they hit it off. Two weeks later, he had a full-time, well-
paid design job that sponsored his visa to work in the United
States. And I had a beautiful book cover—all because he was
crazy enough to talk to a stranger on his bike ride home.

Take your job search beyond email and social media and
look for opportunities everywhere, even when you're biking
down the street. The in-person connections you make will
get you closer to where you want to go.

Try on jobs to see if they fit

Finding meaningful work is all about experimentation, and being open to new opportunities. Remember Kristen, who left her sales job at Google and by pursuing her esthetics certificate, found that she has a gift for doing make-up and making others feel comfortable in their own skin? Or Zack, who taught himself how to code, got a full-time job at a tech start-up and is now developing his second app? Both Kristen and Zack were okay with being beginners. They admitted what they *didn't know* and experimented with a new opportunity to see if it was the right fit.

The job search process is time-consuming, and the last thing you want to do is start a new job and realize a month later that it's not at all what you thought it would be. A great tactic when you're considering a career transition is to try on a job in person to see if it fits before you even apply.

When I was considering other opportunities for after the Peace Corps, one thing I considered was teaching. I researched teaching credential programs, master's programs in education, Teach for America, and New York City Teaching Fellows. I spent countless hours preparing for my Teaching Fellows interview, reading books, and watching documentaries about education. I talked to my teacher-friend Gayle about my job search, and she said, "Smiley, you should just come visit my class next week."

When I visited Gayle's class, not only did I realize

what an amazing teacher she was, but I also realized that teaching (at least in an elementary school classroom) was not for me. I found the smell of the building nauseating and twenty-five kids running around like maniacs made me freak out. By 2:15pm, I was exhausted. I kept looking at the clock to see when class was over, and I realized I had no interest in classroom management, which is a huge element of good teaching. I still care deeply about education. But spending one day in a 4th grade classroom made me realize that being an elementary school teacher is not for me, at least not right now.

Reach out to people that work in environments you're interested in working in. Ask if you can shadow them for the day, or even a morning. Can you picture yourself in their job? Why? Why not? If you're interested in two or more opportunities, test both. If you can't shadow someone, consider interviewing her about the work she does, her environment, and what her day-to-day is like to get a sense of the job.

Seek short-term entry-level experiences

Six months after graduating from college, when I moved to New York City to do freelance work in the film industry, I took any job on a film set I could get. For a few months I worked as a production assistant (or PA, as they're commonly referred to) on several different films. For one gig, my job was to sit on the back of the grip and electric truck, and make sure no one that wasn't part of the crew took anything (like lights or cables) from the truck.

For twelve hours a day, six days straight, in 20 degree weather, I sat on the back of a truck near Bryant Park and froze my ass off for $100 a day. Since the truck was a few blocks away from set, I didn't learn anything about film production. I barely interacted with anyone, except for a few grips who chain-smoked all day and a few tourists who wandered by, asking if anyone famous was in the movie.

On my next gig, I worked for $50 a day as a PA on a small independent film, but told the line producer I didn't want to watch a truck, I wanted to be on-set. Because the film was a low-budget project, they were highly understaffed, and I ended becoming the assistant location manager, helping the location manager and the line producer scout new locations and manage on-set logistics for the film. I saw first-hand how involved making a movie really is.

While I got paid half as much, the experience of being an apprentice on-set taught me infinitely more than making $100 a day guarding a truck. Two months later, my location manager brought me onto another gig as her assistant location manager and paid me $200 a day. After that, I worked for nearly two years doing freelance location work. I learned so much that after two years of freelancing, I produced a short film about a day in the life of two Iraq War veterans struggling with post-traumatic stress disorder. Taking the skills I learned on various film sets, I managed a cast and crew of over 40 people, something I never would have been able to do had I not turned the experience of getting frostbite on my toes into an opportunity for an apprenticeship.

If you're new to a field, look for short-term, entry-level *experiences* in the form of internships, apprenticeships, consulting opportunities, or freelance gigs that offer on-the-ground learning and mentorship from people with expertise. While these experiences may pay less, they can often be much more valuable than entry-level jobs where you do something you already know how to do (like watch a truck, answer a phone, or schedule meetings). The best thing about short-term experiences is that if they aren't the right fit, you can easily move on to something else.

Often the best entry-level experiences are not advertised on websites or job boards. You may have to create one for yourself, like Zack did when he convinced the Vice President of TaskRabbit to give him an internship, or when I told my line producer I wanted to work on-set.

If you're having trouble coming up with an idea for an apprenticeship, check out the Leap Year Project, created by Victor Saad. Interested in going to business school but worried about the cost, Victor created a self-directed, multi-city master's degree in design, business development, and social innovation. He developed 12 different experiences in 12 months for himself, apprenticing with places like a leading architecture firm in Seattle, an art and apparel community in Chicago, and a digital agency in San Diego. Inspired by his leap year, he decided to create an actual school for others to learn by doing, called Experience Institute (details in the Resources section). Victor's story teaches us that it's possible to create any kind of short-term apprenticeship that makes sense for you.

Is Graduate School Worth It?

During a quarter-life transition, many people like Victor face the question of whether to pursue graduate school. There have been countless times over the past eight years that I've been in a bookstore and come *this* close to buying a GRE study guide. But even though grad school has seemed attractive to me at various times during my twenties because I love learning so much, I've never actually taken the GRE or applied to a master's program. This is mostly because the idea of accumulating more debt terrifies me, and partly because I've been interested in so many different things that I never felt committed to pursuing any one degree in particular.

However, I have many friends who have pursued graduate degrees in law, business, medicine, public policy, and environmental management, among others. For some, grad school has been a life-changing breakthrough. For others, it was a costly decision they now regret. The stories in this section will help you determine whether grad school makes sense in the context of your breakthrough.

I have a 30 year-old friend named "Kate" who recently finished law school, passed the bar, and is now making over $150,000 a year (plus bonuses) as a junior associate for a large, prestigious corporate law firm. Not long ago, Kate and I had dinner and she told me, "I wish I had known what I wanted to do before I went to law school, because I knew I wasn't passionate about the law or practicing law. I made a practical decision—I wanted future stability and financial flexibility."

She told me that she had worked till one o'clock in the morning four nights in a row that week, and she was miserable at work. She also mentioned that after a year of studying for the LSAT and applying to law school, three years of law school, hundreds of thousands of dollars of tuition, and a year at her firm, she recently had a realization that she wanted to brighten people's lives by becoming an interior decorator.

"Had I known this then," Kate says, "I would have spent the three years I spent busy, broke and tired in law school, working as an entry-level assistant or floor associate at a home decorating store, apprenticing and taking night classes to get a design certificate. Five years later, I would have been well on my way to being a real decorator instead of pining for it now and wishing I had been smart enough to follow my heart in the first place."

After talking to so many people who went to graduate school for different degrees, I've determined that there are two main groups that people fall into, in terms of why they want to go to grad school. In one group, you have folks that want to learn a new skill set, meet inspiring people who share common interests, and use the degree as a means to align their work with their purpose. In another group, you have people who go to grad school because they don't know what they want to do, are scared to ask themselves what they actually want, want to make money when they're older, and easily be able to answer the question, "So what are your plans now?"

In other words, there are *people who have a clear intention behind why they are going to grad school and people who don't.*

Beyond wanting an intellectual challenge, Kate didn't really know **why** she went to law school. On the other hand, Conor Gleason, another 30 year-old lawyer friend of mine, pursued law school as a means to an end, inspired by his desire to help people who are marginalized in society. After finishing his undergraduate degree, he spent a year volunteering in a poor community in Ecuador as an English teacher and after-school program coordinator. He then went on to work as an investigator at a public defense office for almost three years in New York, helping gather information to defend people accused of crimes.

Conor's interest in law school was inspired by his unique job experiences following college. "I recognized that my capacity to make change and fight for social justice was hampered by my minimal skill set," explains Conor. "A law degree meant more skills, which equated to more opportunity to make change." After attending law school, Conor passed the New York bar, and started working as an immigration attorney for The Bronx Defenders, a public defense office which provides innovative and client-centered criminal defense, family defense, civil legal services, social work support, and advocacy to indigent people of the Bronx.

Conor recently defended a long-time lawful permanent

resident from being deported. He explains, "Congress decided over a decade ago that people convicted of certain crimes—including many non-violent misdemeanors—cannot get bond in immigration proceedings and must remain in detention throughout the course of their case. Our client was in mandatory detention for almost a year while we fought the case; there was essentially nothing we could do to get him out."

After almost a year of hard work, Conor and his colleagues won their case and freed their client from detention. The resident is now back in the United States, reunited with his fiancé and his daughter, both U.S. citizens. "Seeing him out of detention and in street clothes for the first time was amazing. The hug we exchanged was something I will never forget," Conor said.

Though Conor certainly finds his work meaningful, it has been an uphill battle. Unlike some of his classmates who are making at least six figures at corporate firms, Conor is making barely more than $50,000 a year, and he's in $185,000 of debt from law school. When I asked him whether he felt law school was worth it, he told me absolutely it was.

"I think law school is 'worth it' for anybody who is dedicated to learning and gaining insight into how our public institutions and social structures function," he said. "Law school is very hard. It is time-consuming, draining, and it changes your daily life completely. Public interest students face similar pressures as students going the corporate route—there is a tremendous amount of stress and competition in law school, no matter where you go and no matter your goals. You are graded on a curve, and you are ranked—most jobs consider your ranking, where you went to law school, and your experience. Thus, it makes the grueling three years—plus the brutal misery that is studying for the bar—pass by a lot more smoothly if you have a long-term goal in sight."

Provided you have a clear purpose or end-goal like Conor did, grad school can make sense. This doesn't necessarily mean you have to want to stay in the field of your degree for the rest of your life. Conor mentioned that several of his classmates are now working in education, social enterprise, or for tech start-ups. But it does mean you should think deeply about whether grad school will enable your goals and how debt will affect your ability to live your desired lifestyle in the near future. The years of living abroad in Ecuador and working as an investigator allowed Conor to discover *why* he wanted to go to law school. Had he gone to law school at the age of 22, he might not have found the degree as useful.

Another friend of mine, Daniel, is one of the smartest people I know. He has a master's degree in public policy, and an MBA, both from top tier programs. He recently started working for a top management consulting firm, where he makes about $150,000 a year, flies business class all around the country, and expenses his meals. He rarely spends more than three weeks in a row anywhere he goes, and sometimes puts in 16-hour days and 80-hour weeks.

Daniel recently told me that he missed working with

purpose and that he was less fulfilled as a consultant. "Until my current job, I always worked for mission-driven organizations," he explained. "And the missions were usually big, loud, and ambitious (like connecting people through lending to alleviate poverty, when I worked for Kiva in Latin America). The hard part about working as a consultant is that you don't have that big picture to help keep you focused during those inevitable rough patches. The thing that I do get most excited about is working with our clients to help them solve problems. When we can do that, it is gratifying, even if it can be a slow and frustrating process. Many consultants think about this job as an apprenticeship. And if nothing else, I can always say it builds character."

One reason that Daniel is working as a management consultant is to pay off loans from his two master's degrees (which total upwards of $200,000). I was curious whether he thought grad school was worth it, especially given the amount of debt he has. "Yes, 100% yes," he told me. "I met so many amazing people at grad school. Some of them will be friends for life; some of them I've lost touch with already. But everyone I met is incredibly talented, smart, and driven, whether their goal is to solve global warming or to launch the next PayPal. When you surround yourself with dreamers, it forces you to raise personal expectations as well."

Despite his debt, Daniel believes grad school has already opened doors on his journey and he is using this support system to find his next opportunity. If you're considering whether grad school is the right lily pad to leap to next, here are several questions you can ask yourself:

1. Will grad school provide me with a new skill set I need to learn or professional opportunities I don't already have that will help me get closer to my purpose?

2. Will grad school introduce me to a community of people who will inspire me, and support me in reaching my potential? Can I *only* meet this community of people by attending grad school or is there another way to find this community?

3. Is now the right time for me to go to grad school? Do I have enough work/life experience to make what I'll learn valuable? (Recall that Conor lived abroad for a year and worked for over three years before realizing that law school would give him the skills he was lacking.)

4. Is another person in my life (parent, boss, co-worker, friend) pressuring me to go to grad school, or do I really want to go?

5. What lifestyle sacrifices will I have to make in order to pay for grad school? Will having a lot of debt impact my ability to find meaningful work following grad school?

Kate's not the first person to go to grad school and realize that she wants to do something completely different with her life several years later. It's never too late to embrace the journey to leap lily pads, even if that means going from contract law to decorating homes at the age of 30. "I would advise people against going to law school as a catch-all degree," says Kate. "Having a job that pays me a lot of money and is completely unsatisfying has made me realize that it's important to do the thing that you're good at and that you also happen to love. Of course I'm afraid that I won't succeed with my next move. But I'm also excited to finally know what I want to do next, and to truly believe in myself."

REMEMBER

A quarter-life breakthrough isn't about finding the perfect next step or answer, it's about *finding an opportunity, based on your purpose right now, that allows you to make a positive impact in the lives of others.*

Instead of looking in vain for your dream job, start your meaningful job search where your **gifts**, the **impact** you want to have on the world, and your desired **quality of life** overlap. Be aware that you may not be able to address all three of these pieces at once, since finding meaningful work is a balancing act. Clarify your breakthrough priorities by asking yourself what's most important to you. The breakthrough priorities we set for ourselves and the choices we make at a young age determine who we become later in life.

To begin your meaningful job search, look beyond yourself. Signal the noise so others can aid your search, and use the networks of people you don't even know yet. Think of Bernat, who asked a complete stranger for help while riding home on his bicycle. Wherever possible, don't take an entry-level position doing something you already know how to do (like sit on the back of a truck and get frostbite). Seek short-term experiences, internships, or apprenticeships that offer on-the-ground learning from people with expertise.

Graduate school may offer an incredible opportunity to learn new skills, gain expertise, and build a network, which can increase your ability to make an impact in the areas you care about. However, it's important to ask yourself whether now is the right time for you to go back to school based on your purpose, and how having debt will affect your desired lifestyle and limit the choices you have once you graduate.

So far, this book has helped you embrace the journey by starting to think about what you want for your quarter-life breakthrough. But thinking about something will only get you so far. Moving forward, you need to take your breakthrough seriously through concrete, actionable steps. In the next chapter, you'll get your breakthrough hustle on and find the support you need.

When we begin listening to the voice within, the potential we create for ourselves, as well as the possibilities we create for others, are endless.

PART III
ON TAKING YOUR BREAKTHROUGH SERIOUSLY

"You are never strong enough that you don't need help."
-César Chávez

BREAKTHROUGH HUSTLING

In Ted Gonder's "Smashing Fear" talk, there's a moment when he lets the audience know "shit's about to get real." He asks everyone to stand up and take out their notebooks. This is *after* he shows YouTube videos of the honey badger sticking his head into a swarming beehive to extract the larvae, as well as Mike Tyson calmly taking endless jabs to the head only to use his impregnable defense to knock out his opponent with one perfectly-timed, well-placed punch.

Ted asks everyone to rip out a sheet of paper and write down one thing they know they need to do that they've been scared of doing for months. "If you don't write something down," Ted says, "you won't do it." Then, each person exchanges papers with the person next to them, and promises to email in a week, to make sure the other person has accomplished their task.

My one thing that I was scared to do was to start a blog and write my first blog post. I had been telling myself I was going to start a blog for two years, but I had never actually done it. I had been talking about this idea for so long that at one point my buddy Zeb registered a blog domain name for me (GiveMeAFuckingBreak.wordpress.com), under the pseudonym Senator Poswolsky.

When my partner from Ted's exercise texted me the next weekend to see if I had started my blog, I remember thinking to myself, "Shit, she remembered. I'm so screwed." I tried to think of excuses I could tell her that wouldn't make me look pathetic. "My girlfriend was in town visiting this weekend" (wait—I totally mentioned to her I didn't have a girlfriend). "My MacBook is broken" (no—that's ridiculous). "Work is crazy these days" (nope—I had mentioned to her I was bored out of my mind at work).

In the end, I realized it would probably be easier to write the damn blog post, rather than make up a stupid excuse. I went to Wordpress, registered the domain name for whatsupsmiley.com, picked a theme for my blog, and wrote my first blog post about how my best friend Andreas had officially deemed 2012, "The Year of Love." After putting it off for two years, the whole "starting a blog" thing cost me $18 and about twenty minutes of my time.

Looking back now, after writing more than 50 blog posts and numerous pieces for other publications, I can say that writing one sentence on a piece of paper and spending twenty minutes to create the blog changed my life.

The antidote to fear is taking action towards our goals. But how do we take action when we know our goals are changing and that the journey to find meaningful work is not easy, quick, or simple? To put it bluntly: *we hustle*.

If myself, my friends, or my father are any indication, most of us are going to be leaping lily pads to get closer to aligning our work with our purpose for a long time. Recall the story of Alex, who went from writing about the Red Sox in Boston to working for Google in Mountain View, all within six years (and he worked for the Obama campaign, the federal government, and the United Nations in between). This is a reminder that the journey calls for serious preparation: *breakthroughs require both inner hustle and outside help*.

In this chapter, you'll take action by getting your breakthrough hustle on in three phases. First, you'll give yourself the time and space for **vulnerable experimentation**. Then, you'll **plan your breakthrough** and map out your goals. And finally, you'll **build a support system** of people who share your values and believe in your potential. All of the breakthrough hustlers featured in this book did not get where they are today alone. They got there because they found people to help them along the way.

Ideas for Vulnerable Experimentation

Practice self-love

Like many 18-to-34 year-olds who have moved back in with their parents after living on their own, I've moved back home—twice. One time was a few months after graduating from college when I was figuring things out, and another time was when I was 27 and unemployed. Moving back home with your parents has a bad rap. I think of *Seinfeld*'s George Costanza going around New York City, trying to get a date by saying, "I'm unemployed, and I live with my parents."

But it certainly has its perks: saving money on rent, a refrigerator full of food, and getting to spend time with people who love and support you. On the flip side, there's constant pressure to answer the inevitable question, "So, what the hell are you doing with your life?" (or, "when are you getting out of here and have you thought about grad school?").

In my experience, it's easy to get overwhelmed when you move back home, experience fear of failure, and get stuck (especially when you're unemployed). When I was living at home at the age of 27, I was applying to jobs unsuccessfully and feeling like I'd never in a million years have a breakthrough. One night, I went out with a friend who asked me a powerful question: "What do you do every day to take care of yourself?" When I didn't say anything, she pressed me. "How do you practice self-love every day?"

Now maybe it's because I grew up in Boston, where it's 22 degrees all winter long, and a good number of people spend much of their adult lives driving around like madmen and cursing each other, but *self-love* was not something I was familiar with. When I was living in D.C., over-worked and stressed, I *definitely* wasn't taking care of

myself—and I got shingles! I didn't give myself time to eat
well, see friends, meditate, write in my journal, or exercise.
If you don't take care of yourself, it is nearly impossible to
reach your goals or help anyone else reach theirs.

Starting to hustle doesn't translate to finding job
postings online and applying to as many as you can.
Starting to hustle means you spend time doing things you
love, with the people you love. It also means learning how
to be kind to yourself. As my friend Amber Rae, a writer,
entrepreneur, and lifestyle coach reminds me, "When we
optimize for our health and wellness, we can fully share
our gifts with the world." She often asks, *what do you need
on a daily basis to feel like the best version of yourself?*[24]

BREAKTHROUGH EXERCISE

Weekly Self-Love Rituals

Make a list of all the things you love to do every
week that aren't related to work. I've broken
these up into three categories: **personal, social,
and wellness rituals.**

Personal rituals:
(*A few examples: reading* The New Yorker, *going
to the farmer's market, taking photos on a walk.*)

Social rituals:
(A few examples: having coffee with a friend, going out to dinner with your partner, going to a dance party.)

Wellness rituals:
(A few examples: yoga, meditation, running.)

Each week, pick one ritual from each category to incorporate into your weekly routine. Note: these self-love rituals may become part of your desired lifestyle requirements. Consider whether a job that doesn't allow you to pursue these rituals on a regular basis is the right fit for you.

Be true to your needs

I used to think that the way to impress people at happy hour was to tell them exactly what they wanted to hear. When I lived in D.C. and people asked me, "What do you do?" I would answer, "I'm working as a special assistant at the Peace Corps, really enjoying it, gaining lots of valuable experience, and this job is a perfect stepping stone, because I'm thinking about business school next."

To be clear: I used to lie. The truth was I didn't really

want to go to business school. I was actually thinking of becoming a freelance writer. I lied because it's a lot easier to pretend you have your shit together than to be honest. Being honest can be scary. But people can't help you if they don't know what you need. Every time I told someone that things were going great at work and that I was considering business school next, they said, "Oh, that's wonderful—congrats." The conversation would end, and I'd be left clutching a business card, still knowing in my head that I was screwed.

At the StartingBloc program, after my talk with Evan on the rooftop, I participated in the Ideas Marketplace activity, where every StartingBloc Fellow pitches an idea for a project or business to the group. Since I didn't have a business to pitch, I decided to get vulnerable and pitch myself. I told the 98 people in the room—most of them strangers—that I was planning on leaving my job that summer to move to San Francisco, and my writing skills were available for anyone who was interested.

Afterwards, at least 15 different people came up to me and connected me with other people interested in writing and social entrepreneurship. One of those people was Nathaniel Koloc, co-founder of ReWork, who was helping Amber Rae launch The Bold Academy in Boulder, Colorado. We stayed in touch after StartingBloc, and I reached out to him about helping out with the first-ever Bold Academy. Nathaniel invited me to volunteer at Bold that summer, and when the company moved to San Francisco, he and Amber offered me the job to be Bold Academy director.

I got that job because I got vulnerable and shared my needs. If I had lied and told everyone at StartingBloc that I didn't need their help and that I was thinking about business school, I would have arrived in San Francisco with nothing but a suitcase after quitting my job. Instead, I arrived with a network of connected contacts and a future job prospect.

BREAKTHROUGH EXERCISE

Sharing Your Needs and Gives

1. Next time you're at a happy hour and someone asks you, "So, what do you do?" be honest. If you're employed and unhappy at your job, say what you'd rather be doing and what you're interested in doing next. If you're unemployed, say you're unemployed and explain what type of job you're looking for.

2. Next time you host or attend a dinner party, let your friends know you want to try something fun. Tell them you're embracing vulnerability by leading this activity. Hand out two sticky notes to each person towards the beginning of the night. On the first one, have everyone list three things they "need" right now, like job leads, inspiration, a creative project to join, or a long hike. On a second sticky note, have everyone list three things they're able to "give" the group, like web design help, yoga classes, or cooking someone dinner. After everyone is done, put all the post-its on the wall in two separate spaces. Have everyone take a look, and see how they can help others, and what they can learn from others in the room.[25]

Go outside your comfort zone

There's an episode of the popular HBO series *Girls* where Hannah—an unemployed freelance writer living with her best friends in Brooklyn—goes to a job interview at an online publication and asks the editor what she should write about. The editor tells her she should have a threesome and then write about it. Hannah looks at her like she's crazy, explains that she can't have a threesome because she has enough trouble as it is, figuring out where to put her attention on *one* person's body. The editor then shows Hannah a framed image of her comfort zone and an arrow pointing to a circle outside the comfort zone, with the words *where the magic happens.*

Breakthroughs involve change, and many of those changes will probably be outside your comfort zone. Your breakthrough is about experimentation and trying new things to get you closer to your goals. Deepa Subramaniam did just that, with incredible rewards.

Deepa, 31, had been working at Adobe for ten years, ever since she graduated from college. Deepa is very talented, and she steadily worked her way up to becoming a principal product manager, meaning she managed a team of product managers, engineers, and designers to take strategic ideas from conception to execution, quickly and correctly.

During her tenth year at the company, she began to get restless and eager for a career change. "I am not a huge risk-taker. I tend to treat change the way a shy boy might ask out a girl—sniffing around and working up courage before deciding to take action," explains Deepa. "Having hit this huge milestone, a decade at a large and established company, I thought back to what I envisioned for myself when I was in high school and college. I had always seen myself working as a leader within an organization focused on making the world a better place. Though Adobe's mission to empower the creative class with the best tools and services was something I felt passionate about, I was starting to realize that this mission wasn't in total alignment with what I wanted to spend my time and energy doing as I got older."

In order to figure out what her purpose was, Deepa went outside her comfort zone and started making some new friends. "I started talking to more people, younger and older, about what they were doing, how they were doing it, what organizations piqued their interest and so on," she says. "I expanded my social circle outside of my usual 'tech-y' friends, and made a special effort to talk to people of varied backgrounds. This was how I stumbled into the social impact space where many organizations, both non-profit and for-profit, sounded like they could use my particular skills and strengths. The 'light' went off when I realized I was spending more time reading blogs and articles about technology used at the intersection of social change, instead of the web design and web development-focused materials I would normally consume throughout my day."

Around the time she was branching out and trying to learn more about the social impact space, she saw a tweet from charity: water, a non-profit organization bringing clean, safe drinking water to people in developing nations. The tweet caught her eye and landed her on charity: water's "We're Hiring" page, where she noticed an open position for their director of product. Within minutes of reading it, Deepa knew she was the right fit for the job.

"The posting called specifically for someone with my exact skill set and desires," says Deepa. "This job was in the space I wanted to be in, and would be leveraging all of the things I naturally liked to do, and did well."

By reaching out to friends (*using other people's networks*), Deepa found a former charity: water employee, who introduced her to the founder. After she told the founder she was interested in the position, she went outside of her comfort zone even further and got her breakthrough hustle on.

She knew Adobe had a program which provided paid sabbaticals to employees after five years with the company, so she pitched Adobe on letting her use her six-week sabbatical to volunteer for charity: water. Adobe agreed, and Deepa used the time as a way to try out living in New York and working for charity: water. Instead of quitting her job at Adobe, moving to New York and hoping for the best, she used one of our meaningful job search techniques: *she tested an opportunity through a short-term apprenticeship.*

A few weeks into her trial, Deepa discovered she loved working for the non-profit, and that she also loved living in New York. She decided to leave her job at Adobe, and took a significant pay cut to work as charity: water's director of product. While Deepa was initially hesitant to leave a lucrative job at a company she had been working at for ten years (and who wouldn't be?), she made her transition by *taking tangible, incremental steps* towards her next lily pad. First, she started hanging out with people other than her "tech-y" friends. Then, she researched more about the social impact space, using blogs and Twitter to learn about new opportunities.

Then, she *used other people's networks* to get in touch

with the staff at charity: water. Instead of immediately quitting her job and moving to New York on a whim, she tested the new job and new city out with a six-week apprenticeship. After ten years going down one career path, Deepa successfully found a new way of using her skills to make an impact—all because she went outside her comfort zone.

Plan Your Breakthrough

Make a vision board

One evening in Washington, D.C., before I left my job, I came home from a long day at work to find three of my roommates sitting around our dining room table. Katie, Elisabet, and Leslie had laid out a huge pile of (mostly women's lifestyle) magazines, scissors, glue sticks, and colored construction paper.

"Smiley, join us," they said. "We're making vision boards!" In my typical, cynical manner, I laughed at them. "I'm not cutting pictures out of a magazine, what is this, 4th grade? I'm too busy for this Oprah-induced foolishness, I'm gonna check my work Blackberry for the 58th time today."

They proceeded to make vision boards without me. Even my other roommate made a vision board, although his consisted of only a koala bear, a rotisserie chicken, and a giant bottle of beer. I felt kind of left out, so I sat down and awkwardly started looking through the magazines, anxious, not choosing anything to cut out. After five minutes, I got distracted, and gave up. But my roommates pestered me for a week about not making a vision board. Finally, I sat down, alone, deep in serious thought and perused the pages of *Cosmopolitan*.

My vision board for my breakthrough, which I still keep taped to my door, featured pictures of places I wanted to travel and spend time (Barcelona, the woods, the beach, San Francisco), things I wanted to eat and drink (avocado, coffee, popsicles, bowls of pho), activities I wanted to do a lot of (write, read, run, sun salutations), and things I wanted to experience (risk, freedom, change, growth, relaxation), and some random stuff (Michael Jackson dancing). Yes, I cut out a picture from *Glamour* of two people kissing. ("*Glamour*? *Glamour*?!" Yes, *Glamour*.)

You may think it sounds pathetic, a grown man cutting pictures out of a ladies magazine and gluing them to green construction paper. To be honest, it was more profound than pathetic. It was difficult for me, as I imagine it is for most men, to be vulnerable with my emotions. It was difficult for me to take myself seriously. That was the first time I had ever made a vision board, and nearly every single vision on my board came true. Using scissors and a glue stick has a strange way of taking you back to when you were a kid, when creating and dreaming were second nature. Having a breakthrough is beginning to dream again.

Vision Boarding

What are your visions for your breakthrough? Make a vision board by cutting out pictures and words from old magazines. Think of **activities** you want to do a lot of this year, **places** where you want to spend time, and **emotions** you want to feel.

Set a deadline

Shortly after I moved to San Francisco, I was riding my bike home one night when a school bus with a live band playing on it drove by. My friend George Zisiadis, 23, stuck his head of the back of the bus and screamed, "Adam, get on the bus, we're having an all-night moving dance party!"

I was like, "Huh? Dude, I'm biking! What I am supposed to do with my bike?"

"I don't know," George said. "Try to bike onto the bus!" George is crazy. He's also one of the most brilliant people I have ever met. I suppose you could call him an interactive artist, but he calls himself a creator who is passionate about exploring the curiosity and inner child in all of us. He once flooded his bedroom with 3,000 LED-filled, motion-sensitive balloons, for a project called Balloonacy, the world's first-ever interactive balloon immersion. Over 2,000 people, from babies with their mothers to 85 year-olds with hearing aids had a euphoric balloon dance party in his bedroom.

On another occasion, George converted a 20-foot truck into a penthouse apartment celebrating New Year's Eve every ten minutes. Participants were greeted with overwhelming amounts of champagne, party hats, confetti poppers, hugs, kisses, balloons, and a full sound system. In a few hours, over a dozen countdowns were had, with over 500 elated participants—in November.

Why does George do these things? "We grow up indoctrinated to accept the status quo around us," he says. "Seeing my own wacky ideas turned into reality messed with that. It inspired a self-confidence and self-efficacy that I'd never felt before. My whole reality shifted around the realization that the world need not be so static after all."

Indeed. When I first talked about the idea of writing a book, George was the first person to take my idea seriously—before even I did. He asked me one pointed question, *"When? When are you going to write the book?"* The question alone was enough to make me freak out. But I went home and started outlining.

"The first thing I always ask is 'When?' and even 'What time?'" says George. "Having a specific date and time makes your effort real in a way that can't be ignored.

Your projects will be ready when they premiere, not the other way around." In order to accomplish anything, you need to set a deadline. Once you set a date (say, for leaving your current job or launching your next project), your dream is no longer a dream. It's real. It's on the calendar. It's happening. A deadline facilitates short-term and long-term planning, and allows you to take actionable steps towards your goals.

Map out your 6-month breakthrough goals

When I set a date to leave my job, I was stressing about what I was going to do for money after my last day at work, how I was going to find an affordable apartment in San Francisco, and how I was going to find a job when I got there. In order to keep myself from freaking out every night before bed, I mapped out my six-month goals in my journal.

Massive goals can be overwhelming, but when you break your goals down into manageable chunks, achieving them becomes more possible. Appreciate the value of each baby step. You can check out my Breakthrough Goal Map for reference. (You may want to break your map down into week-long chunks, if that makes it easier for you.)

BREAKTHROUGH GOAL MAP

Operation:
Date:

<u>*My breakthrough mission statement:*</u> *In the next six months, I will...*

<u>*My 1-month goal:*</u>
Tasks to accomplish this goal:
People I need to help me accomplish this goal:
Skills I need to accomplish this goal:
Finances I need to accomplish this goal:
Self-Love Rituals I need to be my best self:

<u>*My 3-month goal:*</u>
Tasks to accomplish this goal:
People I need to help me accomplish this goal:
Skills I need to accomplish this goal:
Finances I need to accomplish this goal:
Self-Love Rituals I need to be my best self:

<u>*My 6-month goal:*</u>
Tasks to accomplish this goal:
People I need to help me accomplish this goal:

Skills I need to accomplish this goal:

Finances I need to accomplish this goal:

Self-Love Rituals I need to be my best self:

SMILEY'S BREAKTHROUGH GOAL MAP

Operation: Quit my job in D.C., and find a job in San Francisco!

Date: April 1 - September 1

My breakthrough mission statement: *In the next six months, I will...* leave my current job, leave Washington D.C., move to San Francisco, and figure out a financially sustainable way to pursue my interest in writing, and support young entrepreneurs making an impact.

My 1-month goal: Sit down with my boss, explain my plan to my parents, thank my colleagues for an incredible learning experience while working with them.

Tasks: Schedule a meeting with my boss, have coffee with co-workers

People: Boss, parents, Evan, friends, my sister

Skills: Embrace fear

Finances: Current paycheck, limit expenses to save money

Self-Love Rituals: Run 3x/week, yoga 1x/week, start meditating, daily journaling, talk to my sister, go for a weekend camping trip, dance party, re-watch Season 4 of *The Wire*, eat lots of pho noodle soup

**My 3-month goal:** Have my last day at work, and move out of D.C. apartment.

Tasks: Make last day at work official, tell my roommates I'm moving out, schedule good-bye party, blog 1x/week

People: Boss, HR staff, roommates, all my friends, my sister

Skills: Embrace fear, daily writing practice

Finances: Current paycheck, limit expenses to save money

Self-Love Rituals: Run 3x/week, yoga 1x/week, daily journaling, go to friend's wedding, go to favorite spots in D.C. one last time

**My 6-month goal:** Be living in San Francisco, pursuing writing, supporting social entrepreneurs, and making some money.

Tasks: Buy a plane ticket to SFO, find an afford-able place in SF (god help me), write for at least 3 publications, mentor at StartingBloc, talk to other social entrepreneurs, reach out to other people's networks, find a new job

People: Other writers, other social entrepre-neurs, strangers who live in SF

Skills: Daily writing practice

Finances: Money from a new job to cover SF rent and all expenses

Self-Love Rituals: Run 3x/week, yoga 1x/week, daily meditation practice, daily journaling, ex-plore the beautiful city of San Francisco

Invest in your breakthrough

One Sunday evening when I lived in D.C., I was sitting on a park bench with my friend Meredith. I was telling her how much I was dreading going to work the next day. She was also feeling bored at work, and she told me about a social innovation fellowship program called StartingBloc she had recently applied to. The program brought together motivated young professionals interested in changing the world and the deadline for the next institute was that night at midnight! I rushed home to fill out the application.

A couple months later, when I found out I had been accepted to the program, I began to get really excited, until I realized it cost $1000. I thought to myself: "I'm considering leaving my job, I can't afford to waste $1000 right now." Meredith was also nervous to spend that much money, but we both finally decided it was probably worth spending the money on our careers, as opposed to food or booze.

That $1000 was the best money I've ever spent. I met nearly 100 people who became enthusiastic supporters of my breakthrough. They started following my blog, connected me to other writers and social entrepreneurs in San Francisco, and provided the net I needed to catch me when I leapt. After the program ended, I found writing opportunities through our group's Facebook page, including interviewing entrepreneurs for the StartSomeGood blog, editing a book, and writing for a social impact publication called *Dowser*, which led to me to getting published in *Forbes*.

Investing in your breakthrough doesn't mean you have to spend a ton of money (especially if you're low on savings)—you can also invest your *time*. Remember how I met Nathaniel, ReWork's co-founder, and he asked me to come volunteer at the first Bold Academy? I could have easily turned down the experience because it was unpaid. But I decided volunteering at Bold would be a worthwhile investment of my *time*. In eight days, I met fifteen inspiring young leaders, and numerous staff and mentors, including people who worked at TED, IDEO, and The Unreasonable Institute. Because I was an engaged volunteer, the CEO of Bold Academy reached out and asked me if I'd be interested in running their next program.

So, for the cost of going to StartingBloc, then giving eight days of my time at Bold Academy, I got inspired to have my breakthrough, met several now-close friends, published numerous pieces, and got a paying job allowing me to share my gifts with the world. Was the investment of time and resources worth it? I definitely think so.

Below are several breakthrough investments that offer a high return on investment. While a graduate studies program can certainly be a worthwhile breakthrough investment depending on your long-term goals; the exorbitant cost makes it a lot riskier.

Breakthrough Investments with High ROI

1. Attend a leadership development program or apply for a fellowship program that aligns with one of your current interests. (Note: many of these programs have scholarships available if you need financial assistance.)

2. Attend a conference or event that interests you, like a trade summit, start-up weekend, film festival, maker fair, craft fair, or political conference. (Note: some of these events can be expensive. See if they have a volunteer application—that way you can attend and meet interesting people *for free.*)

3. Enroll in a class or workshop for a skill you want to develop. The class could be online or in-person, and there are plenty of great ones offered through General Assembly, Skillshare, and Udemy, to name a few.

4. Offer your time. Find a short-term internship, apprenticeship, or volunteer opportunity that allows you to meet people, gain experience, and further your breakthrough goals.

Check out the Resources section for specific ideas about these investments.

Building Your Support System

Share your breakthrough with others

Remember how Evan followed up with me after our conversation on the Santa Monica rooftop? He was in Colorado and I was in Washington, D.C., but that didn't stop him from calling me every week to ask if I had "the talk" with my boss yet.

Why did Evan keep calling me? Because I asked him to. I asked him to hold me accountable to what I said I would do. I didn't realize he was actually going to follow through—but that's why finding an accountability partner is so crucial. As soon as you have an idea of what lily pad you want to leap to next, share your idea with people you trust. Ask at least one person to hold you accountable by calling or emailing to check up on you and support you.

When you share your plan with others, you increase your chances of finding supporters who can help you achieve your breakthrough. Building a community of believers is everything. Once you hear Debbie Sterling's story, you'll understand why.

Eleven years ago, Debbie, now 30, was one of only several women in her engineering major at Stanford University. During a three-dimensional drawing class, a male teaching assistant held up one of Debbie's drawings in front of everyone and asked, "Who else thinks Debbie should fail this assignment, why?"

Debbie remembers, "It was so messed up. I cried in the bathroom. It was one of the most embarrassing moments of my life. I knew I could do the drawing, I just needed the foundation, the spatial training they weren't providing. I lacked confidence after that, and I understood why so many women stayed away from engineering."

Women have historically been represented at far lower rates than men in science and engineering, both professionally and in college programs. A mere five percent of first-year female college students intend to major in science, technology, engineering, and mathematics (STEM) fields, and only about ten percent of engineers in the U.S. workforce are women.[26]

After college, Debbie moved away from engineering and interned at a graphic design company in Seattle. Seeking more meaningful work, she volunteered in rural India with the British volunteer organization, VSO. When she moved back to San Francisco with her husband, she found a job via LinkedIn as the marketing director of a jewelry company. She had enjoyed making jewelry in college and was convinced jewelry was her "calling."

After a year though, Debbie grew tired of working in the jewelry industry and became re-interested in what she had studied in college: engineering. With her own embarrassing experience from Stanford imprinted upon her memory, she had an idea for a company that would create more opportunities for female engineers. With friends one Sunday over brunch, Debbie *went outside her comfort zone* and shared her idea to start a toy company to get young girls interested in engineering.

Her friends loved the idea, and told her she had to pursue it. From the living room of her small studio apartment in San Francisco, Debbie created GoldieBlox, a construction set and companion storybook designed specifically for the way young girls learn. The toy helps girls learn spatial skills by leveraging their verbal skills. Debbie's goal was to level the playing field with boys, who learn spatial skills throughout their childhood from a variety of toys like LEGOs, Bob the Builder, and Thomas the Train.

She started prototyping the toy on nights and weekends, and stayed on at the jewelry company for another six months. Why? For starters, she wanted to save money. More importantly though, she was gaining valuable skills in marketing, financial planning, sales, and retail distribution—expertise that she knew would come in handy when launching her own business. As she told me, "I didn't quit my job right away; I treated my job as training for what I knew I was going to do next. I felt like I was getting paid to go to business school."

Eventually, Debbie did leave her job to work on GoldieBlox full-time. She started telling more people about her idea, and the enthusiasm was palpable, so much so that several friends started working for her.

Debbie funded the first GoldieBlox production run on Kickstarter, raising over $285,000 from 5,500 backers. Her toy was featured in *The Atlantic, Upworthy,* and on Good Morning America. It became a huge hit at Toy Faire and Maker Faire, and it's now sold at Toys "R" Us stores across the country. It turns out a whole lot of other people shared Debbie's belief that if women make up half the population, they should also be the ones designing and building the things we use every day.

GoldieBlox did not end up on the shelves of the largest toy store in the world overnight. It got there because about two years ago, when Debbie was still working full-time for a jewelry company, she shared an incomplete and imperfect idea with friends over pancakes. Debbie was willing to put herself and her idea out there. Her idea resonated, and people came flocking to support her and her vision.

Create a Breakthrough Advisory Team

After I finally had "the talk" with my boss, I assembled a small team of mentors, friends, and strangers to support me during my breakthrough.

Whenever I started getting nervous about my upcoming transition, I knew I could reach out to my team for guidance. I selected advisors with experience in the areas I wanted to work in, as well as ones based in San Francisco, which meant that these people were also helping me network for future opportunities. I also selected two members that I had never previously met before, reaching beyond my immediate contacts and expanding my network.

Be selective when assembling your advisory team. Remember: people can only give the advice they know how to give. If you want to pursue a new path, find someone who has experience in that area and who works for the type of organization you want to work for. Deepa was able to find people in a sector where she had few contacts by starting to hang out with people who worked in social impact instead of tech.

You may need to spend some time (after your one-week social media sabbatical) using social media or relevant websites and blogs to find suitable members for your breakthrough advisory team. The search process will help you identify people who share your values and can help you get to the next lily pad. Think of your team like an organization thinks of their board of advisors: the stronger the board, the better the performance of the organization.

Breakthrough Advisory Team

Select five people to join your team. At least two advisors should be people you've never met before. At least two should have several years experience in the area you're interested in pursuing. At least one should be physically based where you live or are planning to live. If possible, include someone at least ten years older than you, and someone younger than you.

Find communities to support your breakthrough

Finding communities of people who share your values and believe in your potential will significantly strengthen your breakthrough. A great example of someone who used her communities is a 26 year-old named Betsy Nuñez, who I met at the Dell Summer Social Innovation Lab in 2012. Betsy, who grew up in a military family, was helping her sister Emily, 24, an active-duty U.S. army officer, prototype her idea for a sustainable fashion company called Sword & Plough.

The company makes stylish bags out of recycled military surplus fabric and creates employment opportunities for U.S. military veterans in their supply chain and manufacturing process. She was really excited about building the venture with Emily, but feeling uneasy because she knew she had to return to her job in marketing and sales with Education First, an international education company, where she'd worked for more than three years.

Seven months later, Betsy attended The Bold Academy, while still working as a sales consultant for Education First. The experience of being around other twentysomethings figuring out their breakthroughs inspired her to embrace her fears and join Sword & Plough full-time.

"While at The Bold Academy, I sat with a mentor who was encouraging, but also eager to ask me hard questions," recalls Betsy. "After talking through my reasons for leaving my job, I realized, that on the other side of the fear was getting what I wanted: seeing Sword & Plough and a mission I believed in, succeed. The moment I knew I had to commit to this fully was when my mentor asked me, "If Sword & Plough is something you 100% want to see succeed, then are you willing to risk not giving it 100% of your time and commitment?"

Less than a month after Betsy left her job to work with her sister full-time, she and Emily launched a Kickstarter campaign, and within two hours of being live, exceeded their $20,000 goal. After a month, they raised over $312,000 from 1,500 backers. Since Emily is currently deployed in Afghanistan, Betsy is now in charge of day-to-day operations at Sword & Plough. To date, the company has supported 35 veteran jobs, recycled over 15,000 pounds of military surplus, and made over 1,700 stylish bags for consumers all over the country.

The only reason Sword & Plough has been successful thus far is because of the community Betsy and her sister built around them. The only reason you're reading this book is because I met people over the past 18 months who pushed me outside of my comfort zone, encouraged me to take a risk, and held me accountable to do just that. If I had hadn't met people like Evan or Ted, I would have easily succumbed to the power of naysayers or haters. To be clear, *haters are anyone who keeps you from pursuing your dream. Everyone going through a breakthrough has to face their haters.*

Haters can be roommates or good friends—it's shitty, but it's true. When I lived in D.C., one of my roommates was also unhappy at work. I kept encouraging him to find work that was meaningful to him. He told me that no one loves their job, and that if it was up to him, all he would do is travel, drink beer, and pursue women. He saw work as a necessity to make money and pass his days. Because of my roommate's attitude, I felt guilty for wanting to find a job that provided meaning in addition to a salary. One of my good friends in San Francisco even told me not to write this book. "I'm pretty sure that kind of book has already been written, like 100 times, by people who know a lot more than you; you're just wasting your time," he said.

Who we spend our time with matters. If the people you're currently surrounding yourself with, either at home or at work, aren't helping you get where you need to go, then you need to find some new friends as soon as possible. Supportive or intentional communities can be groups of entrepreneurs, intrapreneurs, innovators, social changemakers, co-conspirators, artists, teachers, mentors, and friends united in the pursuit of self-empowerment and impact. Your community has your back, makes sure you're following your dreams, and holds you accountable to your goals. *Your community allows you to overcome your haters and have a breakthrough.*

Depending on what you're interested in and where you live, it might be incredibly easy or rather difficult to find supportive communities. Social media may help you find people and groups who are doing things you're excited about, or you may have to reach out to people beyond your network.

Keep in mind that communities don't have to be strictly professional in nature—the important thing is to find people who share your interests. In D.C., I was part of a community called Monday Night Activity Club, which was all about playing capture the flag and having fun on Monday nights. In San Francisco, I'm part of The Passion Co. community, a group of people who commit to completing a 30-day passion project. I'm also part of the Digital Detox community, which believes that it's important to step away from technology every now and then. I was a counselor at Camp Grounded, Digital Detox's summer camp for adults in the redwoods. There, I met tons of interesting people, all because we shared an interest in *Wet Hot American Summer*, camp crushes, star-gazing, and spending a weekend without Facebook.

If you're having trouble finding an existing community in your area, you can try to build one yourself. Remember how Debbie first shared her idea for GoldieBlox—a toy to get young girls interested in engineering—with her friends over Sunday brunch? That was at an "Idea Brunch" that she and her friends organized. Every month, they would gather at a different group member's house and share their ideas. Some people would share ideas for projects or new businesses, and others would simply share what was on their mind. Having that group come together once a month was a big part of what got Debbie moving towards her breakthrough.

BREAKTHROUGH EXERCISE

Community Building

Find 2-3 communities you're interested in joining or learning more about (they could be interest-based, skill-based, or professional networks). Social media and sites like Meetup.com can be excellent resources to find such groups. In the next month, reach out to at least two communities about how you can get involved, and attend their next meeting or event. If you can't find communities in your area that excite you, try building a monthly group meetup yourself, like Debbie's Idea Brunch crew.

REMEMBER

The journey to leap between lily pads and find your next opportunity will never be quick or easy. There is no magic bullet. That's why *successful breakthroughs require both inner hustle and outside help.* First, get your inner hustle on through vulnerable experimentation: practice self-love through weekly rituals, be true to your needs (especially when someone asks you what's going on with you), and go outside your comfort zone. Second, start planning for your breakthrough now: make a vision board, set a deadline, map out your 6-month goals, and invest in your breakthrough.

If all of these things seem overwhelming, pick one or two for now. Finally, sew the net that will catch you when you leap by building your support system: share your breakthrough with others and create an advisory team that will hold you accountable and provide valuable resources. Seek out intentional communities to support your breakthrough, whether it's a professional group or a brunch meetup.

Breakthroughs are about figuring out your next step, as well as surrounding yourself with people who will hold you accountable to your goals. You can't have a breakthrough alone. Your breakthrough is only as strong as the people you have to help you along the way.

In the last chapter, we'll turn to the stories of four inspiring women—doing everything from starting an urban farm in a food desert to leading sustainability efforts for a Fortune 500 corporation—who have applied these techniques in breakthrough hustling to their search for meaningful work. Their stories teach us a valuable lesson: that no matter what happens, failure is impossible, because taking your breakthrough seriously gets you closer to figuring out what you want to give to the world.

GOING ALL-IN

Numerous blog posts and books about quitting your job to "do what you love" or "follow your dreams," mistakenly assume that everyone who seeks meaningful work wants to "go all-in" by starting their own venture or becoming self-employed. While Tom started Rising Tide Car Wash because he was interested in ensuring people like his brother, who has autism, could find employment, and Debbie started GoldieBlox because of the discrimination she faced as a female engineering student, not everyone who wants to make an impact is going to start a new business. If they did, who would work for Rising Tide Car Wash or GoldieBlox? Who would teach math to the 4th graders at Gayle's school or teach all the math teachers how to teach math?

This world needs breakthrough entrepreneurs and intrapreneurs (those working in companies, making change from the inside out). "Going all-in" can involve starting your own venture, but it can also mean sharing your gifts by working for another organization, or splitting your time between getting your side project started and working part-time for a cause you believe in. *"Going all-in" is an indication of how much your work is aligned with your purpose, not whether you are your own boss.* Alex went all-in when he left the Red Sox press box to volunteer on the campaign trail, and Deepa certainly went all-in when she left Adobe after ten years for charity: water, a job 3,000 miles away in a completely new sector.

There are advantages and disadvantages to starting your own venture, as well as pros and cons for working for someone else. In all cases, there'll be some trade-offs you have to make. You have to determine the right balance that provides meaning for you, as well as accept that this balance might change over time.

This final chapter presents the stories of four women entrepreneurs, intrapreneurs, and artists who are figuring out how best to share their gifts with the world. They remind us that there is no simple (or single) answer for finding work that makes you come alive. Each of these women *accepted that there wasn't only one answer, and were willing to explore multiple answers.* Their stories teach us five valuable lessons of breakthrough hustling that will help you find meaningful work now and in the future: **challenge your assumptions, balance your priorities, stay in sync, look beyond your job title, and re-define success.**

Nora Painten: Starting a Student Farm in Brownsville, Brooklyn

Nora Painten, 31, began farming in Connecticut in 2007 (ironically) as a way to delay starting a career, but loved it so much that when she moved to New York City with her now-husband, she was determined to find a way to grow food in the city.

In 2011, she noticed that there were thousands of acres of abandoned lots owned by the city. She found an 8,000 square-foot lot near Rockaway Avenue, in Brownsville, Brooklyn. Across from a large public elementary school, the lot was filled with weeds and trash. Passionate about urban farming and working with kids, Nora reached out to city officials, who gave her permission to develop the lot into a school garden, provided she could raise the funds needed to build it.

Thanks to strangers who also cared about equal access to garden education, Nora raised most of the start-up capital she needed through a $24,000 Kickstarter campaign. She incorporated as a non-profit, and continued to seek project funding by applying for grants.

Over a year later, the Brownsville Student Farm Project offers garden education classes and fresh produce to students at P.S. 323, as well as volunteer farming opportunities for people in the neighborhood. As Nora explains, "There are so many wonderful moments in the garden. I love watching middle-schoolers who arrive with a 'too-cool' attitude gradually lose themselves in the delight of pulling carrots or feeding the chickens. It's also been surprising and wonderful to learn just how many folks in the community have an agricultural history. It seems like everyone who stops by has memories to share of the garden their family kept or the livestock they raised 'back home' on the islands or down South."

"Seeing what we are doing in the garden brings them back and makes them happy. Mothers are always bringing their kids by on a Saturday, when they see us out there working—they are thrilled to see a wholesome opportunity to do some work outside in the neighborhood."

The Brownsville community has welcomed Nora's new venture, but it has not come without hardships. Even though her job feels like full-time, thus far Nora has not been able to afford to pay herself a salary. Her goal is to expand the program to other vacant lots and schools and start an urban farmer training program for people in the neighborhood, but she has struggled to compete for larger grants with other non-profits. Nora is still pursuing additional grants and other ways to monetize the farm, while ensuring produce from the farm ends up on tables in Brownsville. But recently she has started to look for other opportunities to supplement her income.

"Regardless of how things end up with this project, it feels good to have made something tangible," Nora told me. "I know what it feels like to be solely responsible for building something from the ground up. Those are good skills to have and important perspective. And I know the garden has had a positive impact on many people."

Kyla O'Neill: Part-Time Teacher, Part-Time Entrepreneur

Until a little over a year ago, Kyla O'Neill's expertise with jewelry-making peaked with weaving embroidery floss into friendship bracelets at summer camp. After graduating in 2011 with her elementary teaching degree, Kyla, 29, received a bouquet of flowers, which soon began wilting and dropping petals onto her apartment's floor. She noticed one particularly striking petal—the tear-shaped, purple and yellow-striped petal of the Peruvian lily flower, and held it up to her ear as if it were an earring. She began pressing the petals of that bouquet, discovered a means to protect them, and started creating wearable jewelry from nature.

That summer, Kyla shared her new creations with family and friends, wearing them wherever she went. On a trip to Maine, she visited a small boutique. The shop owner noticed her earrings, and inquired about including them in her shop. That moment gave Kyla the validation she needed to turn her creative inspiration into a business.

Once the summer was over, Kyla began her sixth year of elementary school teaching, and continued growing her business, IMPRESSED by Nature, on the side. She took a class at Workshop, a DIY space in San Francisco, called "Getting Your Products Into Stores." Rena Tom, founder of Makeshift Society, a co-working community of creatives, taught the class. In a couple hours on a weekday evening, Kyla learned nearly everything she needed to know about selling her jewelry. At the Renegade Craft Fair, a buyer from the San Francisco Museum of Modern Art Museum Store approached Kyla. Using the skills she had learned in her class, Kyla landed her first large-scale wholesale account.

But she struggled to balance growing her jewelry business with working a full-time teaching job. "When I saw the business grow from selling online on Etsy to selling at local craft fairs and art shows, to selling wholesale to retail shops, I began to consider my options at work," she recalls. "I didn't want to lose the momentum I had, so I pursued part-time work. Fortunately, an opportunity arose at my school to take on the role of extended day director and work 25 hours a week, while also having full benefits."

Kyla is now entering her second year in the part-time position, allowing her the opportunity to both grow a new business that she cares about, while also continuing to work with children, her other love. Her jewelry is now for sale at numerous retail stores throughout the country.

Kyla is considering making the leap to working on IMPRESSED by Nature full-time, but she doesn't want to lose the stability of her part-time job. "Until now, it seemed like my path was fairly clear—I knew I needed to work part-time and had been wanting to take a break from the daily grind of classroom teaching. Now I have an ideal combination of part-time stable work and part-time variable entrepreneurial venture," she says. "In some ways I am afraid to allow my business to grow any more, because it might mean that it will stretch into the only part of my work life that provides consistency—financially and emotionally."

Cassidy Blackwell: A Journey of Natural Hair, Identity, and Self-Expression

During the summer of 2009, Cassidy Blackwell, now 28, was working full-time for a strategic planning firm, when two major changes were unfolding in her life. First, she was becoming increasingly less stimulated and less inspired by her job, leaving her with a bleak sense of purposelessness. Second, for the first time in fifteen years, she wanted to let go of chemical straighteners and wear her natural hair texture.

Eager to find a creative outlet outside of the office, Cassidy started the Natural Selection Blog to document her journey to natural hair. For her, natural hair is less of a hairstyle and more of a lifestyle that celebrates individuality, wellness, self-expression, and education. "There is so much depth to this seemingly surface topic, because for years people of color have had a Euro-centric standard of beauty imposed upon them to the detriment of their physical and mental health," Cassidy told me. "The natural hair movement over the past several years has sparked a revolution of sorts to remake and redefine this idealized standard.

Natural hair has become not only a way for me to express my own identity, but also develop a community of like-minded individuals around the world."

Cassidy began to spend all of her free time outside the office growing her blog, designing, writing, networking, photographing, filming, and doing all of the things she found herself caring deeply about. As the months went on, she grew even less interested in her job, and her performance at work suffered.

"There was one day at work where I let a project detail slip through the cracks," remembers Cassidy. "I let my boss know, and she harshly reprimanded me by saying, 'I don't understand why you're not in crisis mode!' I realized that I wasn't in 'crisis mode,' because I simply didn't care. As awful as it sounds, my work had fallen to so low a priority that I couldn't muster the energy to really give a damn about it. The truth was, it had gotten to a point where I was just collecting a paycheck so that I could fuel this other thing that had become my focus."

Cassidy decided it wasn't fair to her company (or to herself) to stay in her job, and without an exact plan for what she was going to do next, she resigned. "I was confident that whatever instabilities and hardships I would encounter along the way while working on something I was truly passionate about, I would be less miserable than working at that job," she recalled.

Over the next year, Cassidy worked full-time on her blog, partnering with brands and media companies for revenue-generating opportunities like sponsorships, events, and speaking engagements. She grew her blog readership to over 30,000 people, generating over 6,000 Facebook fans and 3,800 Twitter followers. She enjoyed the freedom that came with her new lifestyle. "I could sit on my couch in my pajamas all day or all night, and get my work done," Cassidy boasted. "I had complete control over my schedule, which meant that for about two weeks out of every month, I was on the road working remotely in such lovely locales as Hawaii, New York, and the Caribbean."

Cassidy found meaning from her independent lifestyle and learning how to run her own business, but was soon spending most of her waking hours worrying about money. "Eventually, I realized that what started as a passion project had become a monetized platform and I no longer found the joy and creativity in my blog as I once had," she explains. "Everything—from a vacation to a brunch to a triathlon—became about an opportunity to make money, rather than about my personal desire to do something. My blog was no longer an outlet for my creativity; it was a necessary platform for my survival."

After one year of self-employment, Cassidy started to look for jobs. She realized that from the countless hours working on Natural Selection Blog, she had developed an entirely new set of marketable skills, including content development, social media marketing, and web design. She found a job that was a perfect fit with her new gifts, and got hired to be the social media manager for Stitch Fix, an online fashion company offering personal styling services for women. In her first four months at Stitch Fix, she's already grown the company's social media presence by 300%.

"I put my wishes out to the universe and found a job that was an ideal fit for my new skill set, says Cassidy. "Having the security of my full-time job has removed a lot, if not all, of the pressure of maintaining a fully-monetized blog, which means that now, when I blog, I do it because I love it, not because I get paid. The other main benefit is that I get to work alongside dozens of intelligent and creative people towards a common goal. Each and every day, I learn more about myself. While working independently, a lot of this collaboration and team effort was lost, and all of my ideas were only as big as I could grow them on my own."

Jenni Grant: Artist Turned Fortune 500 Intrapraneur

Jenni Grant, 37, works for one of the largest IT companies in the world, managing projects and programs that reduce the company's global impact on the environment. Her work includes implementing new technology in company buildings around the world so that resource conservation is automated, and maintaining accountability standards through regular tracking and reporting of global energy and water use, waste diversion, and greenhouse gas emissions.

Jenni describes herself as an intrapreneur; her work feels like being at a start-up within a corporation. "I follow a similar process an entrepreneur follows, except I don't work with investors, I work with executives; I don't work on the outside, I work on the inside of an existing structure," she explains. "In a corporation where the bottom line is a priority, there may not be many sustainability initiatives. I have to pitch them. I have to frame sustainability, so that some kind of return on investment is evident. The same goes for innovation. If I want to push for more innovation, the key is demonstrating how innovation creates a net positive impact. I have to get creative and think of every possible form of a return."

In order to pitch her company on promoting electric vehicles, Jenni argued that installing electric vehicle chargers would help attract and retain top engineering talent, who are looking at the perks and services their employer provides. In order to replace fluorescent lighting with LEDs to reduce energy use and CO_2 emissions, she pointed to dollar savings. As she says, "my interest is in protecting the environment, but what I show executives is that I can lower the cost of our electricity bill through the improved efficiency of new lighting technology."

Jenni finds meaning in promoting values she cares deeply about within a large organization that has a large carbon footprint. "My role allows me to fulfill a strong desire I've always had to protect the things in life that provide people with wonder, inspiration, and refuge," she told me. "The most powerful case being nature and the environment. Global corporations can have an enormous, negative impact on the natural environment. By changing the business practices of my company, I can make an equally enormous, *positive* impact. This is incredibly meaningful to me.

One of the most exciting aspects of my job is managing a team of project managers. I love sitting down with them, one to one, and providing guidance on how to be successful with their goals. This is where I get to experience my passion for increasing human potential. We talk about reinterpreting obstacles, strategizing communication, tapping into genius, and creative problem solving."

The reason Jenni has a very influential position, where she has aligned her work with her purpose, is because she *challenged her assumptions* that making a positive difference meant avoiding the private sector. "I grew up thinking I would never work for a corporation," she says. "I began my life as an artist, and even pursued my degree in Fine Arts. But, after years spent in the not-for-profit space working in both arts programming and environmental conservation, it was clear to me that corporations were not going to just disappear. Their power and size was actually growing. I finally realized that there could be incredible reward in transforming these enterprises. If justice and beauty are what drove me, what could have been more satisfying than infiltrating a corporation and rearranging things? And truly, the work of transformation and change is very, very appealing if you are an artist at heart."

Lessons in Breakthrough Hustling

Nora, Kyla, Cassidy, and Jenni's stories offer five useful lessons in breakthrough hustling, that will help make your current or future transition more fulfilling: challenge your assumptions, balance your priorities, stay in sync, look beyond your job title and re-define success.

Challenge your assumptions

Jenni was an artist who cared about environmental conservation, only worked for non-profits, and thought corporations were evil. By trying something new, she found work in the private sector to be incredibly fulfilling and impactful. *Whatever your initial thoughts about a particular job or opportunity, consider the possibility that the opposite could be true.*

Cassidy first challenged her assumption that she needed to build her blog audience only on nights and weekends. She knew when her Natural Selection Blog started to take up so much of her time and energy that she had to leave her day job. Yet she also challenged her assumption again, one year later, questioning whether blogging full-time allowed her to live her desired lifestyle and came to the opposite conclusion: running her own business had placed such a financial and emotional burden on her that it took the fun out of blogging and she was no longer fulfilled.

It's important to challenge the assumption (internalized from many books and blogs) that one needs to make a living from pursuing a passion project. Not everyone interested in crafting is going to start a retail business like Kyla. Most people that blog are probably going to have other jobs to make a living.

I love to write, and so do Cassidy and others in this

book, including Janet, the Airbnb recruiting coordinator and writer. But that doesn't necessarily mean that the only jobs that Cassidy, Janet, or I have in this lifetime are going to be writing. We still have a variety of other gifts to share with the world, and other opportunities may provide meaning in different ways. Both Cassidy and Janet have found meaning at their new jobs, where they work on collaborative teams with inspiring colleagues.

Balance your priorities

These stories teach us the importance of *balance*. As Nora's Brownsville Student Farm Project shows, starting your own venture can change the way a community lives and provide a sense of personal meaning and fulfillment. Potential trade-offs may include burnout, financial sacrifice, and a high degree of emotional anxiety. Depending on your changing priorities (for instance, whether you're raising a family, like Nora is), these trade-offs can drastically change your definition of meaningful work.

You have to accept that how you balance your priorities might change over time. Cassidy enjoyed the freedom and independent lifestyle that came with running her own blog (and who wouldn't, if it meant working from a beach in Hawaii?), but also found this lifestyle to be financially and emotionally unsustainable. And while Kyla has been incredibly successful bringing her jewelry to market and selling nationally at retail shops, she has relied on the stability and benefits that come with having a part-time job at her school.

Remember Janet, who enjoyed her non-profit work helping clients find jobs but recognized when she was bringing too much of her work home with her and when she needed a change? Her full-time recruiting job at Airbnb gives her the work-life balance she was missing in her previous position. By using her free time mindfully, she manages to prioritize her writing and fulfill her desired lifestyle.

Sometimes, in order to determine how to balance your priorities, you may need to leap to a new lily pad (or maybe even two lily pads at the same time) and see what happens.

Stay in sync

When Cassidy decided to stop blogging about natural hair as her means of income, she took the skills she had developed from generating content and building her blog's audience and applied them to becoming a social media manager at an online fashion company. While Jenni certainly went outside her comfort zone by taking a high-level job at a Fortune 500 company, the job wasn't completely out of nowhere: it still reflected her desire to make a positive impact on the environment.

Although Janet leaped to a new sector when she took a recruiting position at a tech company, she was still helping people get jobs; a service she had provided in her old non-profit job. Deepa took the skills she had gained over ten years working in tech as a product manager at Adobe, and applied them to a new role as director of product for a clean water non-profit. Debbie applied the knowledge she gained as the director of marketing for a jewelry company to launching a toy company to get young girls interested in engineering. Alex used his written and oral communications skills to write about baseball, register people to vote, tweet about national security, and write executive briefs at Google.

Even though each person leaped to drastically different lily pads, none of these breakthrough hustlers talked about finding the "perfect job" during their transitions. They simply sought an opportunity in sync with what they were good at and what they cared about. In turn, each found meaningful work.

Remember to refer back to your alignment Venn diagram in Chapter 5, showing your unique **gifts**, the **impact** you want to have on the world, and your desired **quality of life**. Look for that sweet spot, where you have as much alignment as possible.

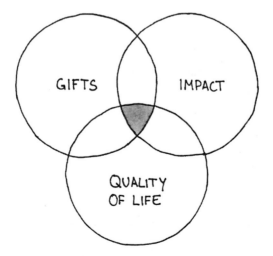

Look beyond your job title

The reason I try to avoid asking people "what they do" within five seconds of meeting them is that I know I'll judge others based on their answer. At Camp Grounded, the summer camp for adults I went to, no one was allowed to engage in "w-talk" (i.e. talk about their job) for a whole weekend. Because of this, after three days, I walked away with countless new friends: some were CEOs, others were Occupy-ers, coders, artists, designers, teachers, policy analysts, musicians, massage therapists, tea makers, or currently unemployed.

Meaning comes from what we do every day, but it's not all about your job title: it's about the people you surround yourself with, the autonomy your work brings you, and the joy you get from your daily life. *Who you work with, the environment you work in, and what you do outside of work* are all contributing factors to fulfillment.

Nora found meaning at the farm by building relationships with local families in Brownsville. Jenni found meaning from being an intrapreneur and craftily pitching energy conservation projects to C-level executives concerned with the company's bottom line. Cassidy found meaning from setting her own hours and being able to manage her blog from Hawaii, but she found a new source of energy and inspiration from working collaboratively with her colleagues at Stitch Fix.

Meaningful work can involve starting your own business and setting your own hours, like Cassidy did with her Natural Selection Blog, but it can also come from working with inspiring colleagues during the day, and then creating something on your own in the evenings. Cassidy isn't getting paid to work on her blog (just as Janet isn't getting paid to write her book), but both endeavors provide a tremendous amount of fulfillment.

Who signs our paycheck, and how much that paycheck is for is rarely what determines whether our job is meaningful.

Re-define success

The stories of Nora, Kyla, Cassidy, and Jenni demonstrate that seeking alignment within a large organization, launching a new venture, and pursuing self-employment are all incredibly challenging. All of these women are still figuring it out. Each is a work-in-progress.

It's hard to say where each will be in a year, let alone five years. But by taking their breakthroughs seriously, each got closer to re-defining success on her own terms. Success is not a front-page news story, a huge paycheck, a venture capital investment, or climbing to the top of a ladder. Success doesn't mean knowing all the answers. Instead, it's starting asking the right questions. *Success is embracing the journey to get closer to what you want to give to the world.*

Success is learning what it's like to be responsible for growing an organization that brings fresh produce to an urban food desert. Success is selling your jewelry at the

SFMOMA Store while running an after-school program. Success is growing a blog into a platform that has inspired women of color all over the world to embrace their identity. Success is enjoying working with your colleagues during the day and enjoying writing by yourself at night. Success is using innovation to ensure a corporation reduces its carbon footprint.

Each of our breakthrough hustlers, just like all of the twenty- and thirty-somethings profiled in this book are drastically different, but all of them have one important thing in common: they've refused to settle for mediocre work. Instead, they've decided to spend their days doing something that inspires them, something that allows them to make an impact that they're uniquely capable of making. If you take your breakthrough seriously enough to take action, and hustle to make your dreams for working with purpose a reality, you can't fail.

CONCLUSION

THE JOURNEY CONTINUES

This past summer, my mom retired as a federal employee, having worked for over thirty years as a nurse practitioner at the Veterans Administration (VA) in Boston. Most of her patients were World War II and Vietnam War veterans, and in recent years, she specialized in hospice and palliative care, improving end of life care for veterans and their families.

I asked my mom what her thoughts were about retirement. Despite her long hours, the stress of working with patients suffering from PTSD, and the challenges of the VA's cumbersome bureaucracy, she told me she was leaving the best job of her life. She said, "It was an enormous privilege to provide comfort for people at a very vulnerable time in their lives—to help relieve their pain and suffering. I feel so truly lucky to have found a career that gave me so much."

Far from a retirement mindset, where she was counting down the days until she could leave her job, she said the work had been so meaningful to her, that after some well-deserved time off, she was going to leap to another lily pad, and continue working in hospice on a volunteer or part-time basis. Whether we have the same employer for over 30 years, or eight different jobs between the ages of 22 and 30, we should all be so blessed to find work that moves us and makes a lasting impact in others' lives.

The journey to find meaningful work never really ends. After I landed in San Francisco, got a job working at The Bold Academy, and started freelance writing, I thought confetti was going to start flying down from the sky. I thought I'd be dancing in the streets every day to Robyn, and I'd never have to think about having a breakthrough ever again. I was wrong.

Recently, a decision beyond my control was made to put The Bold Academy on hold, leaving me without a job or a steady paycheck. Couple that with the fact that San Francisco rent costs nearly as much as college tuition, and that I was recently paid only $40 (two months late) for an article that took me two weeks to write. Now I'm facing yet another career transition, this time at the age of 30. During a quarter-life crisis of the past, I would be probably be freaking out, overdosing on FOMO and hopelessness, and hiding my career change books in a suitcase in the back of my closet.

But after everything I learned this past year from all the twenty- and thirty-somethings you met in this book, I'm not freaking out. Or, rather, I'm not freaking out as bad as I used to—I can at least decide which TV show to watch on Netflix and what size bottle of shampoo to buy.

I'm now able to take a deep breath, and be grateful

for the amazing opportunities I do have and all my wonderful family and friends who believe in me. Rather than compare myself to others on my Facebook news feed and get tormented every three seconds when someone I know gets a new job or moves to Paris, I'm taking small steps to explore my interests. I'm planning on enrolling in a writing class this spring, and creating a class on Skillshare to help others on their journey to meaningful work. I'm listening to the voice within telling me to find work that aligns with my purpose to help others live life to their potential, and researching fellowship and leadership development programs that are hiring for my skills.

I'm embracing my fear of failure, and realizing that the only way to become a better writer is to keep writing. I'm getting my breakthrough hustle on by practicing weekly self-love rituals, exercising, eating well, and spending time with my friends. I'm going outside my comfort zone by spending time with people who work in technology—an area I know very little about. I'm using the support system I built at StartingBloc and Bold Academy to help me find new job opportunities and to remind me to keep dancing.

I'm also looking beyond my job title, and realizing that I get more fulfillment from spending Sunday afternoon with my sister or from listening to my students' stories while volunteering with The Beat Within than I have ever gotten from any job or paycheck. Jumping lily pads, listening to my heart, and beginning to write has made the last year the most meaningful of my life, exposed me to the inspiring people and experiences you read about in this book, and brought me one step closer to the impact I want to have on this world. Refusing to settle and embracing the journey to find meaningful work has helped me discover *why* I'm here—and where I'm going.

In two or five or ten years, you may find yourself bored at work or unemployed, living at the intersection of hopeless, stuck, and FOMO'dosed, and in a similar position you were in when you began this book. And that's to be expected. If the voice goes off in your head alerting you to the fact that something's not working, *listen*. Get clarity on how you want to share your gifts and hustle to make it happen.

I don't know the exact age when the "quarter-life breakthrough" becomes the "mid-life breakthrough" but I'll let you know when I find out for sure—that will be part of the sequel! You're never too old to have a break-through. It's never too late to ask *why?,* and it's always a good time to flip back to the first page of this book.

I hope your quarter-life breakthrough, and the next one, and the next...bring you closer to who you are, the types of people and experiences that make you come alive, and the change you want for the world.

JOIN THE BREAKTHROUGH COMMUNITY

Quarter-life breakthroughs are contagious. Please consider sharing the story of your breakthrough with your friends and community, as a way of sharing the love, and encouraging your peers to embrace their journeys. There are a number of easy (and free) ways to do this:

1. Pass this book on to a friend or stranger who needs to read it.

2. Write a blog post about your breakthrough.

3. Talk about your breakthrough with your friends, family, and co-workers.

4. Host a breakthrough-themed dinner party at your house.

I encourage you to reach out to your fellow breakthroughers for mutual support. I'd love to hear about your own journey too. **Email** smiley@thequarterlifebreakthrough.com or say what's up in any of these places:

Web thequarterlifebreakthrough.com
Facebook The Quarter-Life Breakthrough
Twitter @whatsupsmiley
Blog whatsupsmiley.com
LinkedIn Adam Smiley Poswolsky

BREAKTHROUGH HUSTLERS IN
THE QUARTER-LIFE BREAKTHROUGH

(In order of appearance)

Alex McPhillips
Executive Communications Manager, Google
plus.google.com/+AlexMcPhillips
San Francisco, CA

Kristen McKee
Blogger & Esthetician
courageloveintensity.com
Portland, OR

Evan Walden
President, ReWork
rework.jobs
Denver, CO

Ted Gonder
Co-founder & CEO, Moneythink
moneythink.org |
tedgonder.com
Chicago, IL

Tom D'Eri
Co-founder & COO,
Rising Tide Car Wash
risingtidecarwash.com | *strikingly.com/tom-deri*
Fort Lauderdale, FL

Zack Shapiro
Co-founder & CEO, Luna
useluna.com | *blog.zackshapiro.com*
San Francisco, CA

Gayle Abrams
Math Instructional Coach, Environmental Charter
School and Math Education Consultant,
Math Solutions
Pittsburgh, PA

Ryan Goldberg
Journalist, Self-employed
ryangoldberg.net
Brooklyn, NY

Janet Frishberg
Technical Recruiting Coordinator, Airbnb
and Writer
airbnb.com | *janetfrishberg.com*
San Francisco, CA

Bernat Fortet Unanue
Experience Designer, Yahoo! - Aviate
bernatfortet.com
San Francisco, CA

Conor Gleason
Public Defender, The Bronx Defenders
bronxdefenders.org
New York, NY

Deepa Subramaniam
Director of Product, charity: water
charitywater.org | twitter.com/iamdeepa
New York, NY

George Zisiadis
Artist & Designer
georgezisiadis.com
San Francisco, CA

Debbie Sterling
Founder & CEO, GoldieBlox
goldieblox.com
Oakland, CA

Betsy Nuñez
Co-founder & COO, Sword & Plough
swordandplough.com
New York, NY

Nora Painten
Director, Student Farm Project
studentfarmproject.com
Brooklyn, NY

Kyla O'Neill
Owner & Jeweler, IMPRESSED by Nature and
Extended Day Director, The Berkeley School
beIMPRESSEDbynature.com
Oakland, CA

Cassidy Blackwell
Social Media Manager, Stitch Fix and Founder &
Editor, Natural Selection Blog
stitchfix.com | *Naturalselectionblog.com*
San Francisco, CA

Jenni Grant
Manager, Global Sustainability
and Real Estate Programs
linkedin.com/in/jennigrant
Bay Area, CA

NOTES

INTRODUCTION

[1] "Gallup: State of the American Workplace Report: Employee Engagement Insights for U.S. Business Leaders," *Gallup*, 2013. Retrieved from: www.gallup.com/strategicconsulting/163007/state-american-workplace.aspx

[2] Cliff Zukin and Mark Szeltner, "Net Impact: Talent Report: What Workers Want in 2012," *Net Impact*, May, 2012. Retrieved from: http://netimpact.org/learning-resources/research/what-workers-want

[3] Belinda Luscombe, "Do We Need $75,000 a Year to Be Happy?," *Time* Magazine, September 6, 2010, http://content.time.com/time/magazine/article/0,9171,2019628,00.html.

[4] "Bureau of Labor Statistics, American Time Use Survey 2012," *Bureau of Labor Statistics*, 2012. Retrieved from: http://www.bls.gov/tus/charts/chart1.pdf

[5] Viktor Frankl. *Man's Search for Meaning* (New York: Beacon Press, 2006).

[6] "Young, Underemployed, and Optimistic: Coming of Age, Slowly, in a Tough Economy," *Pew Research Center*, February 9, 2012. Retrieved from: http://www.pewsocialtrends.org/2012/02/09/young-underemployed-and-optimistic/

[7] David Leonhardt, "The Idled Young Americans," *The New York Times*, May 3, 2013, http://www.nytimes.com/2013/05/05/sunday-review/the-idled-young-americans.html.

[8] Annie Lowrey, "Do Millennials Stand a Chance in the Real World?," *The New York Times*, March 26, 2013, http://www.nytimes.com/2013/03/31/magazine/do-millennials-stand-a-chance-in-the-real-world.html.

[9] "Young, Underemployed, and Optimistic: Coming of Age, Slowly, in a Tough Economy." *Pew Research Center*, February 9, 2012. Retrieved from: http://www.pewsocialtrends.org/2012/02/09/young-underemployed-and-optimistic/

[10] Annie Lowrey, "Do Millennials Stand a Chance in the Real World?," *The New York Times*, March 26, 2013, http://www.nytimes.com/2013/03/31/magazine/do-millennials-stand-a-chance-in-the-real-world.html.

[11] Joel Stein, "Millennials: The Me Me Me Generation," *Time* Magazine, May 20, 2013, http://content.time.com/time/magazine/article/0,9171,2143001,00.html.

[12] Richard Ross, *Juvenile In Justice*, 2012. Retrieved from: http://www.juvenile-in-justice.com/

[13] Anup Shah, *Poverty Facts and Stats*, January 7, 2013. Retrieved from: http://www.globalissues.org/article/26/poverty-facts-and-stats

[14] "The Millennium Development Goals Report: 2013," *United Nations*, 2013. Retrieved from: http://unstats.un.org/unsd/mdg/Resources/Static/Products/Progress2013/English2013.pdf

CHAPTER 1: CHANGING YOUR CAREER MINDSET

[15] "24-Year-Old Receives Sage Counsel From Venerable 27-Year-Old," *The Onion*, May 21, 2013, http://www.theonion.com/articles/24yearold-receives-sage-counsel-from-venerable-27y,32515/.

[16] Brad Plumer, "Only 27 percent of college grads have a job related to their major," *The Washington Post*, May 20, 2013, http://www.washingtonpost.com/blogs/wonkblog/wp/2013/05/20/only-27-percent-of-college-grads-have-a-job-related-to-their-major/.

[17] To learn more about the work Nathaniel Koloc is doing to help people build careers worth having, check out ReWork's website http://rework.jobs.

[18] Jeanne Meister, "Job Hopping Is the 'New Normal' for Millennials: Three Ways to Prevent a Human Resource Nightmare," *Forbes*, August 14, 2012, http://www.forbes.com/sites/jeannemeister/2012/08/14/job-hopping-is-the-new-normal-for-millennials-three-ways-to-prevent-a-human-resource-nightmare/.

[19] Robert Safian, "This is Generation Flux: Meet the Pioneers of the New (and Chaotic) Frontier of Business," *Fast Company*, January 9, 2012, http://www.fastcompany.com/1802732/generation-flux-meet-pioneers-new-and-chaotic-frontier-business.

[20] Meg Jay, "Meg Jay: Why 30 is not the new 20," TED video, filmed February 2013, posted May 2013, http://www.ted.com/talks/meg_jay_why_30_is_not_the_new_20.html.

CHAPTER 3: EMBRACING FEAR

[21] Evan Walden, "Make your decision out of love," *Revolution.is*, March 27, 2012, http://revolution.is/evan-walden/.

CHAPTER 4: DISCOVERING MEANING

[22] This section was inspired by the brilliant Teju Ravilochan at The Bold Academy in 2013. Teju is the CEO and co-founder of The Unreasonable Institute, a non-profit which aims to incubate and finance social ventures through world-class mentorship, and thus far

has helped 82 ventures from 37 countries collectively raise over $37 million in funding, and impact over 2,000,000 lives.

CHAPTER 5: ALIGNING YOUR GIFTS WITH YOUR IMPACT

[23] Wendy Kaufman, "A Successful Job Search: It's All About Networking," *NPR*, February 3, 2011, http://www.npr. org/2011/02/08/133474431/a-successful-job-search-its-all-about-networking.

CHAPTER 6: TAKING YOUR BREAKTHROUGH SERIOUSLY

[24] To get more inspiration from Amber Rae, check out her blog at heyamberrae.com.

[25] The first time I ever did a 'Needs and Gives' exercise was at the StartingBloc Institute for Social Innovation (www.startingbloc.org), facilitated by the brilliant Houston Spencer (@houstonspencer). Thank you to Houston for giving me permission to include a version of this exercise.

[26] Catherine Hill, Christianne Corbett, and Andresse St. Rose. "Why So Few? Women in Science, Technology, Engineering, and Mathematics," *American Association of University Women (AAUW)*, February, 2010. Retrieved from: http://www.aauw.org/files/2010/03/Why-So-Few.pdf

RESOURCES

[27] The idea for including a Resources section in *The Quarter-Life Breakthrough* was inspired by the excellent list of resources available in Lara Galinsky and Kelly Nuxoll's book *Work on Purpose* (Echoing Green, 2011).

GRATITUDE

This book would not be possible without the brave twenty- and thirty-somethings who inspired this project, and shared their stories with me. To all of the breakthrough hustlers featured in this book: thank you for refusing to settle, thank you for being vulnerable, thank you for being you.

To the 518 people in 38 countries around the world who supported my Indiegogo campaign, and the good people who work at Indiegogo: thank you for empowering this dream. This book exists because of you.

To my talented editor, Caroline Kessler: thank you for helping me see the tiny speckle of beauty in the pile of shit that was my first draft, and encouraging me every step of the way, all the way to the seventh draft and beyond. More than an editor, you've been a mentor and a compatriot, and this project would have never been finished without you.

To my book designer, Sumeet Banerji: thank you for your beautiful work. Without you, I would have only a Word doc. To Bernat Fortet Unanue: thank you for inspiring the cover design and for stopping to talk to me that day on your bike. To Kara Brodgesell: thank you for following your dream to be a photographer and for your keen eye throughout our shoot in Bernal Heights. To Sydney Malawer: thank you for advising me every step of the way.

To my StartingBloc family, all over the world: thank you for waking me up, thank you for changing my life. To my Bold Academy family: thank you for making me see what's possible when people come together to pursue their potential. Whenever I have a rough day, or think something's not possible, I remember that first night in Alamo Square Park, blasting Macklemore's "Can't Hold Us" and jumping up to the ceiling.

To my Peace Corps family: thank you for your incredible service, and for teaching me what it really means to make an impact. I may have left the agency, but I'll never stop believing in the mission to promote world peace and friendship.

To my Wesleyan family and the Ruby crew: thank you for teaching me how to love life. I may not have learned how to find a job in college, but I sure learned how to find friends that make me happy, which is a tad more important.

Most importantly, thank you to my family. Mom and Dad: thank you for believing in me when I told you I wanted to be Mister Rogers, play for the Red Sox, be a filmmaker, be a writer, and believing in whatever it is I tell you I want to be next. Becca: you inspire me, I love you more than the world. Gran and Grandma: thank you for teaching me how to laugh, I miss you every single day.

We only get to where we are because of those who carry us. To that end, thank you to everyone who has carried me on my journey thus far, from Cambridge, to Middletown, to Brooklyn, to Buenos Aires, to Region 7, to D.C., to San Francisco. You know who you are. I love you and am forever grateful.

Adam Smiley Poswolsky
San Francisco, California

RESOURCES

Here's a list of resources that can help you on your journey. (Note: this list includes resources that I found helpful during my breakthrough, as well as ones that have been recommended by friends.)[27]

BOOKS ABOUT TWENTYSOMETHINGS

20-Something Manifesto: Quarter-Lifers Speak Out About Who They Are, What They Want, and How to Get It **By Christine Hassler.** New World Library, 2010.

The Defining Decade: Why Your Twenties Matter—And How to Make the Most of Them Now **By Meg Jay.** Twelve, 2012.

Twentysomething: Why Do Young Adults Seem Stuck? **By Samantha Henig and Robin Marantz Henig.** Plume, 2012.

BOOKS FOR INSPIRATION

Bird by Bird: Some Instructions on Writing and Life **By Anne Lamott.** Anchor, 1995.

Drive: The Surprising Truth About What Motivates Us **By Daniel H. Pink.** Riverhead Books, 2009.

How to Change the World: Social Entrepreneurship and the Power of New Ideas **By David Bornstein.** Oxford University Press, 2004.

How to Find Fulfilling Work **By Roman Krznaric.** Picador, 2013.

Man's Search for Meaning **By Viktor Frankl.** Beacon Press, 2006.

So Good They Can't Ignore You: Why Skills Trump Passion in the Quest for Work You Love
By Cal Newport. Grand Central Publishing, 2012.

The Art of Non-Conformity: Set Your Own Rules, Life the Life You Want, and Change the World
By Chris Guillebeau. Perigee, 2010.

The Artist's Way: A Spiritual Path to Higher Creativity
By Julia Cameron. Tarcher, 2002.

The Freelancer's Bible: Everything You Need to Know to Have the Career of Your Dreams – On Your Terms
By Sara Horowitz and Toni Sciarra Poynter. Workman Publishing Company, 2012.

The Gifts of Imperfection: Let Go of Who You Think You're Supposed to Be and Embrace Who You Are
By Brené Brown. Hazelden, 2010.

The Purpose Economy
By Aaron Hurst. Russell Media, 2014.

The Startup Guide: Creating a Better World Through Entrepreneurship
By Ryan Allis. 2014.

The War of Art: Break Through the Blocks and Win Your Inner Creative Battles
By Stephen Pressfield. Black Irish Entertainment, 2011.

Walking On Water: Reading, Writing And Revolution
By Derrick Jensen. Chelsea Green Publishing, 2005.

What Color Is Your Parachute? 2014: A Practical Manual for Job-Hunters and Career-Changers
By Richard N. Bolles. Ten Speed Press, 2013.

Work on Purpose
**By Lara Galinsky and
Kelly Nuxoll.** Echoing
Green, 2011.

CAREERS & INTERNSHIPS

B Lab

www.bcorporation.net
A non-profit organization
dedicated to using the
power of business to solve
social and environmental
problems. Awards B (beneficial)
Corporation certification to
for-profit organizations that
meet certain standards of
transparency, accountability,
sustainability, and performance,
with an aim to create value
for society, not just shareholders.

Bridgespan

Bridgespan.org
Provides a free nonprofit job
board and tools to help non-
profit organizations build
strong leadership teams and
individuals develop careers as
non-profit leaders.

Commongood Careers

www.commongoodcareers.org
A mission-driven search firm,
committed to supporting
the recruitment and hiring
needs of innovative non-
profits.

Echoing Green

www.echoinggreen.org
Global non-profit that
provides seed funding
and technical assistance
to emerging social
entrepreneurs with ideas
for social change. Also
posts a monthly list of job
opportunities at impact-
driven organizations around
the world.

Elance

www.elance.com
A place to find, hire, manage,
and collaborate with online
freelancers, offering access
to over 2 million skilled
freelancers from around the
world.

GameChangers 500

gamechangers500.com
Lists the world's

top purpose-driven organizations and profiles organizations that are reinventing the world and redefining the rules of business around fun, fulfillment and fairness to all life.

Idealist
www.idealist.org
Connects people, organizations, and resources to help build a world where all people can live free and dignified lives.

MediaBistro
www.mediabistro.com
Jobs and recruiting, as well as classes, community, and news, for social media and traditional media professionals.

NetImpact
www.netimpact.org
A community of more than 50,000 student and professional leaders creating positive social and environmental change in the workplace and the world.

ReWork
www.rework.jobs
Connects exceptional professionals with companies that are making the world a better place.

CROWDFUNDING & DIY TOOLS

Awesome Foundation
www.awesomefoundation.org
A worldwide network of people devoted to forwarding the interest of awesomeness in the universe. Distributes a series of monthly $1,000 grants to projects and their creators.

Indiegogo
www.indiegogo.com
An international crowdfunding site where anyone can raise money for film, music, art, charity, small businesses, gaming, theater, and more.

Kickstarter
www.kickstarter.org
The world's largest funding platform for creative projects. Helps bring creative projects to life.

MyProject

www.myproject.is

Engages your network while you turn your ideas into reality.

StartSomeGood

startsomegood.com

A crowdfunding platform for non-profits, social entrepreneurs and changemakers to raise funds and grow a community of supporters.

Trevolta

www.trevolta.com

Enables travelers to submit their extraordinary ideas for expeditions in order to raise funds for it.

FELLOWSHIP PROGRAMS & FUNDING OPPORTUNITIES

Ashoka

www.ashoka.org

A global organization that identifies and invests in leading social entrepreneurs – individuals with innovative and practical ideas for solving urgent social problems.

Atlas Service Corps

www.atlascorps.org

A 12-18 month professional fellowship offered three times a year for non-profit leaders from around the world. Fellows serve full-time at non-profit host organizations either in the United States or Latin America working on issues that complement their expertise.

Dell Social Innovation Challenge

www.dellchallenge.org

Identifies and supports promising young social innovators who dedicate themselves to solving the world's most pressing problems with their transformative ideas. Provides university students with world-class teaching and training, as well as with start-up capital and access to a network of mentors and advisors.

Do Something

www.dosomething.org

Encourages young people to create their own vision for

making a difference in their community and provides them with the resources and support needed.

Echoing Green

www.echoinggreen.org
Global non-profit that provides seed funding and technical assistance to emerging social entrepreneurs with ideas for social change.

Fulbright Program

www.iie.org/fulbright
Sponsored by the U.S. Department of State, Bureau of Educational and Cultural Affairs, the Fulbright Program provides funding for students, scholars, teachers, and professionals to undertake graduate study, advanced research, university teaching, and teaching in elementary and secondary schools.

Global Citizen Year

www.globalcitizenyear.org
Forges a new educational pathway for America's emerging leaders by immersing a diverse corps of Fellows in developing countries during a "bridge year" after high school, preparing them for success in college, careers, and the global economy.

Kairos Society

www.kairossociety.org
Selects the most innovative engineering, science, design, business, and entrepreneurship students from top universities in each region of the world to create pioneering solutions that will push the world forward.

Mobilize

www.mobilize.org
Empowers and invests in millennials to create and implement solutions to social problems.

Points of Light Civic Accelerator

www.pointsoflight.org/civic-incubator
Invests in and supports seed stage social ventures that solve pressing social and environmental issues by engaging people.

Presidential Management Fellows Program

www.pmf.gov

A prestigious paid government fellowship for recent graduate students who seek a two-year fellowship in a U.S. government agency.

Thomas J. Watson Fellowship

www.watsonfellowship.org

A grant that enables graduating college seniors to pursue a year of independent study outside the United States.

Thiel Fellowship

www.thielfellowship.org

Brings together some of the world's most creative and motivated young people, and helps them bring their most ambitious ideas and projects to life. Fellows are given a no-strings attached grant of $100,000 to skip college and focus on their work, their research, and their self-education.

Unreasonable Institute

www.unreasonableinstitute.org

A non-profit organization that aims to incubate and finance social ventures through world-class mentorship, and thus far has helped 82 ventures from 37 countries collectively raise over $37 million in funding and impact over 2 million lives.

FINANCIAL PLANNING

LearnVest

www.learnvest.com

Empowers people everywhere to take control of their personal finances so that they can afford their dreams.

Mint.com

www.mint.com

Website that pulls all your financial accounts into one place so you can set a budget, track your goals and do more with your money, for free.

ReadyForZero

www.readyforzero.com

Provides online, personal

financial management tools
for paying off debt.

SKILLS & EDUCATION

Code Academy
www.codeacademy.com
Learn to code.

Coursera
www.coursera.org
Take free online classes from
80+ top universities and
organizations.

Experience Institute
www.expinstitute.com
A 12-month higher education
program that partners
with companies, creative
workshops, and conferences
to place students within real
world learning experiences.

General Assembly
generalassemb.ly
Learn from top practitioners
of programming, business,
and design. Courses are
available in eight cities
across the globe, as well as
online.

iTunesU
www.apple.com/apps/itunes-u
Puts complete courses and
the world's largest online
catalog of free education
content on your iPad, iPhone,
or iPod touch.

Khan Academy
www.khanacademy.org
A non-profit educational
website that provides
free content in math, art,
computer programming,
economics, physics, chemistry,
biology, medicine, finance,
history, and more.

Skillshare
www.skillshare.com
Learn real-world skills from
incredible teachers, online
and in-person.

TechShop
www.techshop.ws
A chain of member-based
workshops that lets people
of all skill levels come in
and use industrial tools and
equipment to build their own
projects.

SUPPORTIVE COMMUNITIES, PROFESSIONIAL NETWORKS & LEADERSHIP DEVELOPMENT

Be Social Change

besocialchange.com

A team of passionate community-builders on a mission to educate and connect the next generation of social entrepreneurs and changemakers creating bold, innovative social impact.

Digital Detox

thedigitaldetox.org

An organization dedicated to creating balance in the digital age. Produces device-free events, as well as workshops, retreats, Camp Grounded (summer camp for adults), and corporate trainings to bridge the gap between disconnecting and connecting.

Generation Progress

genprogress.org

Formerly Campus Progress, Generation Progress educates, engages, & mobilizes a new generation of young progressives.

Global Leadership Lab

www.globalleadershiplab.org

Convenes, develops, and supports a global network of leaders committed to systemic transformation.

Global Shapers Community

www.globalshapers.org

A network of hubs developed and led by young people who are exceptional in their potential, their achievement, and their drive to make a contribution to their communities.

GOOD

www.good.is

A global community of people and organizations working towards individual and collective progress.

Hive

www.hive.org

Educates and connects extraordinary purpose-driven

leaders age 21-39 to create
an abundant and sustainable
world for all.

Impact Hub
www.impacthub.net
Offers you a unique
ecosystem of resources, inspiration, and collaboration
opportunities to grow the
positive impact of your work.

Institute for
Compassionate Leadership
*instituteforcompassionateleadership.
org*
Takes leaders on a journey
where you discover your
purpose for creating
meaningful change in today's
world. Six-month training
program offers executive
coaching, mentorship
and tools to become a
compassionate, self-aware leader.

Meetup
www.meetup.com
Helps groups of people
with shared interests plan
meetings and form offline
clubs in local communities
around the world.

New Leaders Council
www.newleaderscouncil.org
Works to recruit, train and
promote the next genera-
tion of progressive leaders.
NLC recruits Fellows from
outside traditional power
structures and equips them
with the skills necessary
to be civic leaders in their
communities and work-
places.

New Organizing Institute
neworganizing.com
A community of organizers,
committed to solving the
biggest challenges that stand
in the way of change. Trains
organizers to build and
manage effective moments
by integrating tried-and-
true community organizing,
cutting-edge digital strategy,
and data-driven decision
making.

Roosevelt Institute
Campus Network
www.rooseveltcampusnetwork.org
As the first student-run policy
organization in the United
States, empowers young people

as leaders and promotes their ideas for change.

StartingBloc

www.startingbloc.org

Brings together entrepreneurs, activists, educators, and innovators struggling to create change. Hosts transformative 5-day Institute for Social Innovation where Fellows learn from proven changemakers, are pushed to take bigger risks, and find new life-long allies.

The Bold Academy

www.boldacademy.com

A life accelerator program designed to give you the clarity, courage, and community to lead the life you've always wanted to live.

The OpEd Project

www.theopedproject.org

A social venture to increase the range of voices and quality of ideas we hear in the world. Increases the number of women thought leaders contributing to key commentary forums.

The Passion Co.

www.thepassion.co

Inspires, enables, and supports a world where people are honoring their dreams by hosting classes and events centered around engaging in their passion.

Women 2.0

women2.com

A media company at the intersection of women, entrepreneurship, and technology. Creates content, community and events for aspiring and current women innovators in technology.

VOLUNTEER SERVICE & CIVIC ENGAGEMENT

AmeriCorps

www.nationalservice.gov/ program/americorps

Engages more than 80,000 Americans in intensive service each year at non-profits, schools, public agencies, and community and faith-based groups across the country.

AVODAH: The Jewish Service Corps

www.avodah.net

Engages Jewish young people to become lifelong leaders for social change through a year of full-time work at an anti-poverty organization.

BUILD

www.build.org

Uses entrepreneurship to excite and propel disengaged, low-income students through high school to college success.

City Year

www.cityyear.org

An education focused non-profit organization that unites young people of all backgrounds for a year of full-time service to keep students in school and on track to graduation.

Code for America

www.codeforamerica.org

A non-profit that connects citizens and governments to design better services, and supports a competitive civic tech marketplace.

Design Corps

designcorps.org

Creates positive change in traditionally underserved communities by using design, advocacy, and education to help them shape their environment and address their social, economic, and environmental challenges.

Peace Corps

www.peacecorps.gov

Volunteer program run by the United States government. Volunteers collaborate with local communities in 65 host countries in areas like education, youth development, information technology, and the environment.

Serve.gov

www.serve.gov

A nationwide service initiative that enables individuals to find volunteer service opportunities in their community, as well as create their own "do-it-yourself" projects.

Volunteer Match

www.volunteermatch.org
Strengthens communities by making it easier for good people and good causes to connect. Offers online services to support a community of non-profit, volunteer and business leaders committed to civic engagement.

VSO

www.vsointernational.org
Offers volunteers the chance to work abroad to fight poverty in developing countries.

Worldwide Opportunities on Organic Farms (WWOOF)

www.wwoof.org
Organization assisting those who would like to work as volunteers on organic farms internationally.

Youth Service America (YSA)

www.ysa.org
Working with young people and their adult mentors, YSA improves communities by increasing the number and diversity of young people serving in substantive roles.